Cults,
Terror, and
Mind Control

Cults, Terror, and Mind Control

Raphael Aron

Bay Tree Publishing, LLC
Point Richmond, California

© 2009 Raphael Aron

Author's Note:

The inclusion of a particular group or organization in this book does not necessarily mean it meets all the definitions of a cult or terrorist organization, but rather that Cult Counselling Australia, has received inquiries about it or that it has been discussed in the media as having cult-like characteristics.

Library of Congress Cataloging-in-Publication Data

Aron, Raphael.
  Cults, terror, and mind control / Raphael Aron.
      p. cm.
  Includes bibliographical references.
  ISBN 978-0-9801758-2-0
1. Cults--Psychology. 2. Terrorists--Psychology. 3. Brainwashing.
I. Title.
  BP603.A75 2009
  153.8'53--dc22

                                    200902426

Contents

Acknowledgements

The publication of this book would not have been possible without the input of numerous people from all corners of the world. To all of them I extend my thanks and appreciation.

First and foremost to my wife, Shani, who continues to support my involvement in this complex field of work. It is not possible for me to express my true appreciation for Shani's patience or her willingness to accommodate the frequent travel, the after-hour calls, and the day-to-day pressures of this often very unorthodox work.

To my children who are only too familiar with packed suitcases and telephone calls from airports far and wide. It is my hope that the impact on our family life will be outweighed by their increased awareness of the preciousness of each individual's life.

To my mother, Toni, whose love of books inspired me to put pen to paper and write this book. To the memory of my late father, Zev Akiva, who taught me how to read and appreciate the written word.

To Ursula Rembach, my administrative assistant, for her untiring efforts with the extensive research required for this book.

To the police for their assistance in responding to cult-related enquiries. To the media for their interest in this field of work and their interest in bringing these issues to the attention of the public.

To the authors and publishers in Australia and overseas who have granted permission for me to quote from their works in the writing of this book.

To Dr. Gabriel Weimann of the University of Haifa for granting me permission to quote from his research on the use of the Internet by terrorist groups. To Guy Nasuti for granting me permission to quote from his work in relation to the Hitler Youth.

To the multitude of journalists and researchers who have assisted me in learning about the complexities of terrorism and its impact on family and community.

To David Cole of Bay Tree Publishing for his encouragement to pursue this project. To his staff for their invaluable assistance in bringing the manuscript to publication standards.

To the numerous clients who have sought and continue to seek assistance through Cult Counselling Australia. Their strength and determination are an inspiration for so many individuals and families who are frightened and overwhelmed by the intensity and complexity of the issue of mind control and its potentially catastrophic ramifications.

It is my hope that this book will shed light on an important issue. In addressing the cult and terrorist phenomena, we must remain mindful of the preciousness and sanctity of life. If, as a community, we can remain focused on the values of tolerance and mutual respect, we are better placed to face the challenges that confront us and so look forward to a more peaceful and harmonious world.

—Raphael Aron

Introduction

"America's current war on terrorism is perilously flawed without a powerfully-executed, inoculative and preventative educational program on the tactics of mind control and destructive cults.

"The Al Qaeda terrorist network is, at its core, a religious cult that is also manufacturing mind controlled cult martyrs and terrorists. These terrorists and martyrs have become of a similar mind to those people that played out the tragedies in Jonestown, Hale-Bopp and in the Aum Shinrikyo attacks."[1]

When my book, *Cults: Too Good To Be True*,[2] was published in 1999, no one could have predicted the events of September 11, 2001 that in a matter of minutes changed the world and introduced terror onto the doorsteps of modern society. As the Flights UA175 and AA11 crashed into the Twin Towers not only did the New York skyline change forever but so did the security and safety of mankind on planet earth.

At the same time, the terms brainwashing and mind control[3] took on a frightening relevance and meaning as society struggled to understand the motives and the reasoning of nineteen suicide terrorists, educated individuals from middle-class families, who perpetrated these acts.

In October 2002, a group of terrorists wreaked havoc and destruction upon the small tourist community of Bali. The composure of the terrorists during their court hearing—in particular the ringleader of the group who came to be known as the smiling terrorist—attracted the wrath of victims, and the world at large.

The shocking attack on a public school in Beslan, Russia, in September 2004 was significant because it represented the first terrorist attack that specifically targeted children, resulting in the deaths of 196 children.[4]

In July 2005, the world again struggled to understand the motives of a group of London-based terrorists who were responsible for a series of bombings that brought the city to a standstill. Teachers, professionals, and family men had perpetrated the worst act of bloodshed on British soil since World War II. Social scientists struggled to understand the means by which young and idealistic individuals could be radicalized.

In his first address after the 9/11 bombings, President Bush described those responsible as the cult of Al Qaeda. Since that time numerous mental health experts and social scientists have debated the link between mind control and terrorism. Cult expert Steve Hassan writes, "Members of terrorist organizations are in fact members of a destructive mind control cult. The use of influence techniques to create a fanatic is essentially the same. There are many similarities between the ways people are programmed in a cult which can result in an act of suicide bombing. Many people while in a destructive cult, including myself, can tell you that we were ready to die for the cause, if necessary."[5]

These terrorist acts also produced a sense of global vulnerability, which in turn provided fuel for a range of churches, cults and sects to attract new members. At the same time, numerous organizations around the globe offered themselves as havens for the frightened and fearful

Indeed, according to Hassan, following the 9/11 attacks, Scientologists in the guise of mental health professionals gained access to relatives and friends of those missing in New York and Washington, D.C. [6] The Church of Scientology also managed to get its National Mental Health Hotline telephone number broadcast on a cable news network. Michael M. Faenza, President and CEO of the National Mental Health Association (NMHA), said that Fox News had been broadcasting an 800 help line for "National Mental Health Assistance" but the network was unaware that the number was being answered by the Scientologists' center in Los Angeles.[7]

Other organizations heralded the events of 9/11 as proof that the world was coming to an end. Doomsday soothsayers had proof that their dark and evil predictions were all about to materialize. Paul Crouch of the Trinity Broadcasting Network, a Christian media company, said the attack was the next stage in what Jesus described as "the beginning of sorrows" during the end times. New York minister David Wilkerson said the attacks were a warning of a greater destruction he had already predicted unless New York City repented. These messages may have been extreme, but the audiences for them were in the mainstream, according to polls.[8]

Whereas cults and mind control were once a niche concern, the events of 9/11 have since catapulted these issues into the forefront of society, demanding that we find an effective means to safeguard our children and future generations.

This book addresses the connection between cults, terror, and mind control. In particular, it explores the similarities between the mind control techniques used by cults and the means by which terrorist organizations recruit, radicalize, and retain their members. This is not to suggest that groups which are often referred to as cults advocate terrorism. Most of these groups, although misguided and potentially dangerous, would never condone acts of terrorism or murder. Nevertheless, the similarity in the recruiting techniques used by terrorists and cults is highly significant as are the profiles of some of the people who become involved in these groups. This is important; if governments and lawmakers are to be effective in their fight against terrorism, they need to understand the recruitment process and the thinking that energizes it.

When I commenced working in the field thirty years ago, books such as *Snapping: America's Epidemic of Sudden Personality Change*[9] broke new ground in introducing the world to the concepts of psychological manipulation, mind control, and personality change. Even so, at the time the public was skeptical about these ideas.

Since then, the body of information has grown, professional organizations have arisen, and eminent professionals have endorsed the works of others who have studied the mind control phenomenon and its widespread ramifications. Journals, periodicals, and a range of books, from both a professional and a lay perspective, have become available. Extensive research material on the connection between cults and terrorism can be accessed in libraries or via the Internet. The establishment of standards and criteria by which groups can be assessed has lent further strength to the connection between cultism and terrorism.

While the issue of mind remains contentious, an increasing body of evidence supports the notion that the human mind is vulnerable to a process of involuntary change through orchestrated indoctrination.

The continuing growth of cults and sects coupled with the frightening impact of terrorism across the globe are a reality that we can no longer afford to ignore. The thousands of online terror sites are a frightening reality. Ironically, the growth of terrorism since 2001 has placed a spotlight on mind control and the techniques used by these groups.

As young people attempt to make sense of the post-9/11 world, parents and families are justifiably concerned about the possible influence of cults, terrorist organizations, or extremist movements on their loved ones. Multi-level marketing organizations, personal development groups, and a range of fundamentalist fringe churches have also increased their sphere of influence. While the implications of allegiance to any of these groups may vary considerably, the common denominator is the exploitation of an individual and its ramifications.

On a broader scale, the growth of cults and the spread of terrorism are symptomatic of significant gaps in community life and society. Extremist behavior serves to highlight alienation, marginalization, loss of identity, and the need to belong as major issues of our day. At the same time, the meaning of spirituality and the role of religion have been subjected to gross forms of misinterpretation by ideologies that exploit individuals.

While parents, religious and community leaders ponder these issues, governments and lawmakers face huge challenges in containing the growth of cults, the spread of terrorism, and the expansion of many other exploitative organizations. Understanding the nature of these phenomena is an essential step towards addressing these ominous developments.

1

The Evolution
of Cults
and Terror

During the mid-1970s, I was a student at Melbourne University. My interest in counseling took me to the chaplaincy, where I would spend a few hours a week speaking to the counselors and, where possible, sitting in on a number of sessions.

It was during the final examination period in 1974 when I received a phone call from a distraught mother who claimed that her daughter had become involved in a cult. She wanted to know what to do; to whom could she talk? Unsure about how to handle it, I set up an appointment, hoping that in the meantime I could research this intriguing problem. My efforts were fruitless and frustrating. There was hardly a person I could speak with who knew anything about cults. Several people suggested I try to establish contact with American counseling agencies, but I wasn't sure where to start. Others suggested I speak directly with the group which was allegedly hiding this girl.

A week later a second call came through. This time it was about a woman who had left her husband and two young children to travel to India to see a guru. She had left no contact address or phone number, and her husband and brother were very concerned.

It would be an understatement to say that these two phone calls changed my life and, I believe, the lives of many people I have worked with since. As a believer in the concept of Divine Providence, I was unable to ignore these calls and decided to look further into this seemingly very powerful phenomenon of cultism—a force seemingly so potent that it appeared to be able to split families and destroy relationships.

In my initial research I discovered numerous groups which were operating on the fringe of society. Other groups appeared more conventional, at least in their outer appearance. The first step on that journey was the opportunity for me to witness and experience these groups. I was not yet in a position to judge whether these groups were operating in a cult-like manner. I studied Transcendental Meditation, attended the Hare Krishna temple, was audited by Scientology, and meditated at Siddha Yoga. Later on I participated in a program with the Children of God and went fundraising with the Moonies.

I attended conferences in the United States and subscribed to numerous magazines, journals, and press clipping services. The more I researched the phenomenon of cultism, the more my eyes were opened to the complex and intricate nature of these groups that were often labeled destructive. It became clear that the public, the media, and the clergy had underestimated the nature and extent of cults. I saw that the damage inflicted by cults on their members appeared to point to a specific psychological phenomenon often referred to as mind control and called for special attention.

The Jonestown tragedy in 1978 was a significant turning point in awakening the world to the danger of destructive groups. The world was shocked by the sight of more than nine hundred bodies rotting in the South American sun, a testimony to the brave new world that Jim Jones had promised his followers. Subsequent cult-related tragedies strengthened the argument that cults and mind control needed to be confronted.

On a personal level, discovering the cult world was a bizarre experience. I had assumed that cult groups all followed gurus and masters who were living in India or high up in the Himalayas. The word "cult" conjured up images of chanting, meditation, vegetarian diets, and celibacy. It came as a shock to discover that my ideas hardly scratched the surface of this relatively new phenomenon. I learned that there were numerous groups that did not display any of these characteristics but were, nevertheless, destructive and dangerous.

I discovered that, quite apart from the better-known Eastern cults, there were numerous Christian groups that gave serious cause for concern. There were, in addition, a growing number of personal development groups attracting attention because of their methods of recruiting and maintaining trainees in their grasp.

The range of groups, the nature of their beliefs, and their practices were as diverse as their memberships. I found it incredible that people could be attracted to so-called philosophies that preached death and suicide. I was fascinated by the differences between these groups. Some practiced celibacy, while others encouraged promiscuity and free sex.

As my client-base began to grow, I was amazed to find that the followers of these movements were often seemingly well-adjusted and successful members of the community. The belief systems of these organizations were as relevant to the university lecturer as they were to the untrained laborer.

I met people brought up in traditional families who had thrown out their moral codes within days of joining a cult and who were prepared to lie and fabricate stories without hesitation. I saw how their relationships changed dramatically. As values were transformed and reframed, I saw how loving parents came to be seen as enemies.

I discovered that the love and care offered by many of these organizations was wholly and fully dependent on the allegiance the member or devotee gave to the cult. The moment that allegiance wavered the individual was jettisoned from the cult. Ironically, it was that experience that often brought home the truth about the cult's motives.

I found that many clairvoyants, psychics, and fortune tellers were using the same methods employed by the cults. It was also clear that there were no government controls to curtail these peoples' activities or to make them accountable. Many of these operators used the now discredited notion of repressed memory syndrome to suggest that their clients had suffered various forms of abuse earlier in life which they had since forgotten or denied.

I recognized that in order to bring these people home it would be necessary for both them and their families to understand the nature of mind control. I learnt that exit counseling was a process to reverse the mind control and psychological manipulation that had been practiced on innocent cult victims. I discovered that exit counseling was a process which had been refined from the earlier practice of deprogramming, which often involved the use of force to remove a cult member from a group.

Rehabilitation was a long-term process that could take years. Undoing the significant damage caused by some of these organizations required ongoing counseling and therapy. In many instances this process exposed the vulnerability that led to recruitment in the first place. It also exposed the issues that contributed to the person's vulnerability. As the former member began the process of rebuilding his life, these issues still required attention.

But none of these challenges could be compared to the powerful yet elusive effects of mind control. Many cult members seemed to be under a spell or in some sort of trance though they might behave normally. This was a far deeper phenomenon that affected every aspect of their existence, emotional, psychological, spiritual, and financial.

Learning about these issues led me to establishing a grassroots taskforce to address this problem and deal with it. Staffed by volunteers, its goal was to research cultism and assist families who were affected. As a non-denominational group, it served the broader community, providing information and resources as well as counseling and support to families concerned about the fate of their loved ones.

The challenge to continue this work became even more compelling following the terrorist attacks on New York and Washington in September 2001. There appeared to be frightening connections between the notion of mind control and the behavior and mindset of young idealistic people who had been transformed into terrorists, mass murderers, and suicide bombers. Not one of the nineteen perpetrators of the terrorist attacks in the United States had a criminal record in any country.[10]

I watched as social scientists and researchers scrambled to understand the events of 9/11 and the motives of a group of educated people from middle-class families who wrought destruction, creating fear and uncertainty about the future.

Tragically, in the years since, similar terrorist activities have been repeated over and over across the world, in Bali, Madrid, London, Pakistan, India, and the Middle East. And they continue today.

I have learned that there are many different types of terrorist groups. In particular, there are significant differences in the constitutions and the operations of religiously motivated terrorists as compared to secularly motivated terrorists. It is important to understand these differences as the world seeks the means to curtail their activities.

It is particularly disturbing to note that in a post-9/11 world, the event of a suicide bombing no longer attracts the attention it once did. Instead, the phenomenon of a human bomb has somehow become an acceptable tool in the arsenal of extremist groups. Instead of expressing outrage, the community appears to accept that some parents will rejoice in the death of their children as products of the cult of martyrdom.

I have watched as the Internet continues to allow terrorist groups to maintain a global constituency aimed at transforming common people into active participants. Extremists are using the Internet not just to radicalize but to recruit, organize, train, raise and move money, plan, and even execute attacks. Prosecutions and convictions in Europe for terrorist-related offenses almost all involve an element of Internet use of this kind.[11]

Nevertheless, at the same time, the Internet has the potential to neutralize the hatred of terrorist organizations. Opportunities exist for governments to deconstruct terrorist myths and challenge their philosophies of death and martyrdom.

I have observed the frustration of governments as they discovered that there are no simple solutions either to terrorism or the radicalization of young people. Even as religious and community leaders view this phenomenon as a wake-up call, it is clear that there is something amiss in our family structures and social fabric leaving a dangerous vulnerability in our youth.

Cult Counselling Australia was established in 1991 to provide a formal structure for responding to cult issues and their accompanying challenges. The organization now offers a wide range of services throughout Australia and overseas, including direct assistance to families and concerned persons, research, and liaison with other professional groups, various government statutory organizations, the police, and the media.

It is well over thirty years since I commenced this work. In that time I have worked with hundreds of individuals who have become involved in cults. Nevertheless, despite significant changes in how cults present themselves and how they are perceived, I find myself dealing with the same fundamental issues: the psychological and emotional harm inflicted on unsuspecting individuals who join these groups, the hurt to their families, and the resulting destabilization of society.

Over the years, I have witnessed the pain of families being torn apart, the trauma of not knowing the whereabouts of a loved one, and the grief arising out of a cult-related suicide or terrorist attack. I have also been part of family reunions and reconciliation, the re-establishment of relationships and the restoration of individual freedom. These positive outcomes have provided the inspiration to continue an important task that commenced as a result of two phone calls more than thirty years ago.

Cults: An Overview

> "Some human beings seem to be driven by an overwhelming urge to espouse a cause and, failing to find one, may become fixated on astonishingly inferior substitutes. The instinctive need to be a member of a closely linked group fighting for common ideals may be so strong that it becomes inessential what these ideals are and whether they possess any intrinsic value."[12]

Although the cult phenomenon is not something new, the pain inflicted by cult groups and organizations and the frustration incurred in trying to curtail their activities remain very real. Families, friends, community, and religious leaders continue to seek adequate responses to a growing number of cult organizations and fringe churches. As the number of groups and their membership grow, the efforts continue to halt this disturbing trend and to provide assistance to those individuals who have been caught up in these groups.

Within this context, parents and friends often question whether their loved ones are simply involved in a process of spiritual experimentation that ought to be tolerated. At the same time they cannot help but wonder if there is something more sinister and potentially dangerous about many of these groups.

The situation is often complicated by the fact that although a number of eminent scholars have elaborated on the features of groups that appear to operate in a cult-like manner, there is no official professional body that is able to designate a group a cult. There will always be an element of subjectivity in assessing whether a group should or should not be termed a cult.

When the word cult is used, people commonly picture a Western woman donning a sari, or someone changing his name to a Sanskrit or Biblical alternative, or dropping out of school or quitting a job. This image may also include a major and seemingly inappropriate financial commitment and a possible total breakdown in family communication. It is rare, however, to see all these changes demanded by one group, and many groups that may in other ways qualify as cults may show none of these outward signs.

What does lie at the heart of the cult experience, however, is the process of psychological manipulation that costs an individual the freedom to make independent decisions. Victims become increasingly dependent on the cult's system, authority, and environment, essentially substituting this new orientation for their family of origin and earlier belief system.

Though the popular image of cults involves a religious sect of some kind, there are many other types of groups which appear to operate in a cult-like manner. Some psychotherapeutic and personal development groups create situations that are no less cult-like than those created by some swamis and gurus in ashrams and temples. Claiming to offer inner happiness, better business acumen, or improved social skills, some of these groups operate in a manner that clearly exploits the members or participants. Because some of these groups do not present as religious or spiritual in nature, the innocent participant may be at greater risk of being duped and eventually controlled.

In an article titled "Cults Not Gone, Just Mainstreaming,"[13] Marcia Rudin, Director of the International Cult Program of the American Family Foundation[14,] describes a wide variety of cults that attract followers by offering mind-empowerment, psychotherapy, business opportunities, and political activism. Rather than promising spiritual salvation or enlightenment, these groups skillfully market themselves to a new clientele of affluent, often well-established people, by offering financial success, happiness, social success, and self-fulfillment.

"Cults are so sophisticated today," says the mother of a member of the Church Universal and Triumphant. "It's not like it used to be with the Moonies on street corners with flowers. They now like pin-striped business suits. Cults are big organizations."[15]

In more recent times, the exploitative and opportunistic use of alternative medicine by untrained practitioners has also been a cause for concern. Quite apart from the damage done to the reputation of the genuine workers in these fields, using methods of control and domination often very similar to those used by cult leaders, these charlatans have selfishly and often dangerously taken advantage of their positions to harm well-meaning and unsuspecting clients. Documented cases of split families and broken marriages resulting from these practices are a direct result of the lack of control and standards in this growing industry.

Concerns have been raised regarding the cult-like techniques used by multi-level marketing organizations such as Amway to attract recruits and maintain their allegiance. Some multi-level marketing organizations appear to adopt an almost evangelical and cult-like approach, suggesting that involvement in their marketing programs will affect the participants' quality of life and sense of purpose. Other issues of concern include the creation of a sense of dependence on the organization, as well as the discouragement of creativity and individuality.

Channeling is also a common thread of inspiration in many cults. The founder lays claim to a mystical experience, where he or she communicates with a spirit who identifies itself. This spirit is either an individual who has died and "evolved to a higher state," or is a heavenly being such as an Angel.

The idea that a physical, embodied human being can communicate information from an outer source and different dimension of reality has attracted considerable interest. As the messages of entities like Lazaris, Ramtha, and Seth are channeled down to earth, there is concern about the impact of this phenomenon and its similarity to the behavior found in some cults.

It is also significant that some of the earlier known groups are re-emerging with new names and a new profile as the new name can have the effect of disguising the true nature and identity of the group. The Children of God are now called The Family International, Rajneesh has been renamed Osho, and the Aum Shinri

Kyo terrorist cult is called Aleph. Indeed the infamous Aum cult responsible for the 1995 Tokyo subway chemical attacks is a prime example of how a cult can rebuild itself and continue to operate.

According to Andrew Marshall, co-author of *The Cult at the End of the World: The Terrifying Story of the Aum Doomsday Cult*, Aum's revival is astonishing. Not only has it survived its years in the wilderness, but it is expanding again at an alarming rate. In the year 2000 it had about two thousand followers, including five hundred hard core devotees living in cult-owned facilities. It is distributing millions of booklets in which new recruits explain how Aum teachings have given them supernatural powers. It even has its own pop band, called Perfect Salvation, which performs songs written by the guru himself.

A general overview of cult activity over the past thirty years serves as evidence that cults have been active across the world in all sectors of society. Although the format and modus operandi of some groups may have changed, the presence and growth of cults continues unabated.

An early public spectacle of the cult phenomena involved the gruesome murders of Sharon Tate and others orchestrated by Charles Manson in August 1969. The tragedy shocked the world and forced people to question what inspired young successful people to surrender to a charismatic figure.[16]

The dramatic kidnapping of Patricia Hearst by the Symbionese Liberation Army in 1974 received wide publicity. Eventually Patricia joined the SLA in Los Angeles. Following her capture and arrest, Patricia faced the courts. The basis of the defense presented by her lawyers was that "what Patricia did wasn't what she wanted to do but what she had to do." Mind control was now on the public agenda.

However it was the suicide of more than nine hundred followers of the charismatic cult leader Jim Jones in November 1978 that thrust cults into the international spotlight. The images of the bodies of hundreds of men, women, and children rotting in the jungles of Guyana were powerful. The tragedy, which included the death of

276 children, highlighted the seriousness of the cult issue and also galvanized popular opinion.

In September 1984, 750 people became sick after eating in restaurants in The Dalles, Oregon. Investigators later learned that Bhagwan Shree Rajneesh, the leader of the nearby religious commune of Rajneeshpuram, had ordered followers to spread salmonella bacteria in restaurants in order to influence local elections. The event was thought to be a trial run for a larger attack, and "resulted in the largest outbreak of food borne disease" in the United States that year.[17]

In Russia, a would-be Messiah by the name of Vissarion managed to attract five thousand followers as part of his effort to prepare for the end of the world. According to reports in the Russian press, the leader was a former traffic cop who was fired for his drinking. In 1989 he announced that he was the Son of God. He spoke of the "coming end" and instructed his believers that suicide was not a sin.[18]

That same year in Delaware County, Pennsylvania, the Church of First Love was the subject of complaints by residents when members set up homes surrounded by high weeds, oil barrels, and abandoned cars. Some members of the church were selling their property for a planned move to the wilderness to escape an expected nuclear holocaust.[19]

In 1993, the world was shocked as the Waco tragedy unfolded with the eventual death of eighty-three men, women, and children at the Branch Davidian headquarters in Texas. Fixated on biblical prophecies of disaster and the end of the world, the cult began interpreting weather changes as proof of the coming of Armageddon. A blizzard was regarded as an apocalyptic sign, as David Koresh continued to predict the imminent end of society.

In 1994, fifty-three members of the Order of the Solar Temple died in what appeared to be a mass suicide that took place simultaneously in Switzerland and Quebec. Later that year, in December, a further sixteen people, including three children, were found in the charred remains of a remote Alpine village. Farewell letters were left by members stating that they believed their deaths would be an escape from the "hypocrisies and oppression of this world."

The Order of the Solar Temple, or International Chivalric Organization of the Solar Tradition, believed that a death by fire meant reincarnation in the Sirius star system. This pseudo-Templar group attracted many influential people and is still in operation despite the mass deaths in 1994. While anticipating the imminent end of the world due to an environmental catastrophe, some members decided that they should leave the earth prematurely and transit to a better world.[20]

In 1995, the infamous Japanese Aum Shinri Kyo cult (now known as Aleph) orchestrated a sarin gas attack on Tokyo's subways which killed twelve and injured more than five thousand commuters. Despite the attempts by some to downplay the severity of Aum's activities, the Aum attack has the distinction of being the world's first mass chemical terrorist attack. The group built a vast arsenal of biochemical and conventional arms, including mustard gas, anthrax, botulism, Q-fever, sarin nerve gas, and TNT. Aum also experimented with seismic weapons designed to trigger cataclysmic earthquakes in Japan, an idea dismissed by geologists but taken very seriously by the U.S. and Soviet militaries.[21]

In 1997, the world was shocked by the suicide of thirty-nine members of the Heaven's Gate cult. Heaven's Gate members believed that by renouncing all worldly pleasures as well as sex, drugs, alcohol, their birth names, and all relationships with family and friends, the cult members could ascend to space shedding their "containers" (bodies), and enter God's Kingdom.[22] The sighting of Hale-Bopp, an unusually bright comet, was the sign that they were supposed to shed their earthly bodies and join a spacecraft traveling behind the comet that would take them to a higher plane of existence.

Also in 1997, Australian authorities expressed concern about an organization called the Order of St. Charbel in rural Victoria, run by William Kamm, who called himself the Little Pebble. Kamm made a series of apocalyptic forecasts: Perth would be devoured because of the sins of the Sodomites; Sydney would be destroyed by earthquakes and the atomic bomb; the east coast of Australia would be swamped by the sea.

In a leading newspaper report, the Catholic Church was reported as having declared Kamm a fake. In a "global press release" Kamm told followers to remain inside for seven days, cover windows with black plastic, and leave animals outside. "We believe that before the year 2000, the world will be chastised through a comet—possibly two; then the Pope will leave Rome and die soon after, and a third world war would occur."[23]

In early 2000, 780 followers of a Ugandan cult, the Movement for the Restoration of the Ten Commandments, perished in a devastating fire, and a series of poisonings and killings. These were either suicides or an orchestrated mass murder by sect leaders after their predictions of the apocalypse failed to take place.[24]

In February 2005, Tamotsu Kin, the sixty-two-year-old former head of the Central Church of Holy God, was given a twenty-year prison sentence in a Kyoto District Court for sexually abusing seven young female congregants. The presiding judge declared that the abuse had left the girls mentally scarred and described the crimes—twenty-two separate charges involving sexual offenses against girls as young as thirteen—as extremely malicious and unprecedented.

In November 2007, cult followers in central Russia's Penza Region dug a shelter and stocked it with food in anticipation of the imminent apocalypse. The cult leader threatened that the whole group would commit suicide if the authorities attempted to enter the underground shelter. In May 2008, nine survivors left their Ural Mountains hideout after officials had found the bodies of two women who died in the cave.[25]

Also in November 2007, a raid involving four hundred police

resulted in the arrest of the remaining thirty female members of the Japanese Kigenkai sect in Komoro, a quiet town in the country's central Nagano Prefecture. Sect members were accused of subjecting sixty-three-year-old fellow cultist Motoko Okuno to an hour-long ordeal of kicks and punches that led to her death. Among those rounded up were four teenagers, two of them junior high school girls.[26]

In April 2008, Texan authorities removed 418 children from the polygamous Fundamental Church of Jesus Christ of Latter Day Saints. Claiming that the children had been emotionally and sexually abused, the authorities placed them with foster families pending further investigations. The case caused a fierce debate between law enforcement authorities, civil libertarians, the church, and the community.

Cults are well known for seeking sites or outposts where they will not be exposed to public scrutiny or the media. In Australia cults have also been responsible for death and suicide. Children have been separated from their families, and drugs have been administered to helpless patients without consent. Families have been torn apart as a result of the invasive and destructive agendas of cult organizations. Quiet countryside retreats have shielded numerous groups originating in the United States and Europe that have regarded Australia as a haven in which to establish themselves. The Aum cult acquired a large ranch in outback Australia to serve as their refuge once the apocalypse (whether naturally occurring or due to their own efforts) came about.[27]

While focusing on those who commit murder or die at the hands of a cult, it is critically important not to ignore the thousands upon thousands of families who have been ripped apart as a result of the influence of these groups. Young people gone missing, marriages and relationships destroyed, families split apart, individuals who have lost their sense of purpose—these are the legacies of many organizations.

Cults are destructive because of the level of control they wield over their followers. Whereas most social systems and families involve various degrees of control and accountability to authority, cults cross a critical line that ultimately involves loss of freedom, independence, and free choice.

Terrorism: An Overview

"The events of September 11, and the continued threat of terrorist acts in the United States, has the effect of eroding the social, economic, mental, and physical health of our nation. For a small percentage of individuals, the psychological effects are a serious problem needing immediate attention. A majority of individuals continue to function, but sustain low levels of anxiety and depression which will accrue more serious effects down the road if not addressed now.

"Recent scientific studies reveal that psychiatric morbidity associated with mass violence and terrorism can affect large numbers of people, lead to chronic long-term medical and psychiatric illness and cause premature death among the elderly. Studies also link low-grade depression/anxiety with lower effectiveness of the auto-immune system."[28]

While terrorist organizations have been in existence since the beginning of recorded history, their impact has become more apparent in recent decades. In 1970 the Black September Organization used the high visibility of the Olympics to publicize its views on the plight of the Palestinian refugees. Eleven Israeli athletes were murdered during the games.

In October 1974 terrorists wearing uniforms of the Israeli Defense Force took hostage hundreds of pupils in a grammar school in the northern city of Ma'a lot and demanded the release of imprisoned colleagues. At the end of a terrible massacre, twenty-two children and five adults were killed and many others wounded.

In October 1983 terrorists bombed the Marine Battalion Landing Team Headquarters at Beirut International Airport, killing 241 U.S. military personnel and wounding more than 100 others. One of their objectives was to instill a sense of fear in the American people and the U.S. Congress. Their success gave terrorists a major victory. The bombing drove the military from its peacekeeping mission in Lebanon and provided a blueprint for attacking Americans.

"There's no question it was a major cause of 9/11," said John Lehman, a former secretary of the Navy and member of the 9/11 Commission. "We told the world that terrorism succeeds."[29]

The United States and the United Kingdom have published a list of more than forty terrorist organizations operating in various parts of the globe that includes separatist, nationalistic, revolutionary, political, religious, social, and domestic organizations. They range from lesser known groups such as Saved Sect or Saviour Sect, which disseminates materials that glorify acts of terrorism, to arguably the most notorious global terrorist organization, Al Qaeda.

Another organization is the Kach group, which in 1994 was listed by the U.S. State Department as a terrorist organization. Kach is a hard-line Israeli militant group that advocates the expulsion of Arabs from the biblical lands of Israel. According to the U.S.-based Council on Foreign Relations, Kach, as well as the splinter group Kahane Chai ("Kahane Lives"), condones violence as a viable method for establishing a religiously homogenous state. The group has not staged a large terrorist attack since 1994, although people affiliated with the groups have been arrested for "low-level attacks" since 2000, according to the State Department's 2006 Country Report. In 2006 a U.S. Federal Court upheld an appeal that Kach was rightly listed as a terrorist organization. Israel outlawed Kach and its offshoot Kahane Chai in 1994, a month after a Kach supporter shot and killed twenty-nine Muslim worshippers at a West Bank mosque.[30]

The nature of the terrorist group is significant in that it determines the degree to which the group will do harm. For example, groups with secular ideologies and non-religious goals will often attempt highly selective and discriminate acts of violence to achieve a specific political aim. They may choose to keep casualties at the minimum amount necessary to attain their objective. They do this both to avoid a backlash that might severely damage the organization, and also maintain the appearance of a rational group that has legitimate grievances.

In contrast, religiously oriented and millenarian groups typically attempt to inflict as many casualties as possible. Because of their apocalyptic frame of reference, they view loss of life as irrelevant, in fact, the more casualties, the better. Losses among their co-religionists are of little account because such casualties will reap benefits in the afterlife. Likewise, they see non-believers, whether they are the intended target or collateral damage, as deserving of death, and killing them may be considered a moral duty.

The bombing of the U.S. Embassy in Kenya in 1998 inflicted twenty casualties on the local inhabitants for every member of the U.S. personnel. There was an even greater disparity in the proportion of wounded. More than five thousand Kenyans were wounded by the blast. Fear of backlash in such an instance is of no concern as it is often a goal to provoke overreaction and thus widen the conflict.[31]

The difference between secular and religiously motivated terrorists can also be understood by way of example when comparing the violence perpetrated by the IRA with religiously motivated terror groups. Bruce Hoffman, author of *Inside Terrorism*, has referred to the IRA's success against the British government as non-lethal terrorism. "They issued warnings, in some cases they disrupted mass transit, they had big bombs planted in downtown areas which they pulled in on Saturday morning." He compares this activity to the 9/11 terrorists who bombed the World Trade Center or the Oklahoma City Murrah bombing when, in both instances, everybody was arriving for work. "I think it is because of the legitimization and justification of liturgy that creates a mentality out of religious order that anybody is a fair target."[32]

Quite apart from the nature of a terrorist group, there are numerous other factors that are important in any attempt to define and understand terrorism. These include the psychology of terrorism, the history of terrorism, and the types and effects of weapons of mass destruction or disruption used by the terrorist groups. In addition, the roles of the military, government agencies, and volunteer groups in responding to terrorist threats are significant factors as are the terrorists' profile, the psychological consequences of terrorism ,and the treatment of special populations such as children and older adults. Most of these issues are beyond the scope of this book.

More significant in relation to this book are the techniques used by terrorist organizations to radicalize and recruit their followers, taking young, idealistic individuals and turning them into murderers. This pattern appears to have become a hallmark of those organizations responsible for bloodshed throughout the world.

Almost every terrorist attack since 9/11 has highlighted the involvement of educated individuals from middle-class homes. Many were responsible family members who were also holding down stable jobs at the time of the attack. Others were involved in admirable community projects. According to Ami Pedahzur, associate professor in the Department of Government at the University of Texas, between 1999 and 2004 there were three and a half times as many suicide terrorist attacks worldwide as had occurred from 1938 to 1998. Since that time, the attacks have continued unabated. A review of these events reads like a litany of horror.

The U.S. State Department reported that in 2006 terrorist attacks worldwide shot up 25 percent, particularly in Iraq where extremists used chemical weapons and suicide bombers to target crowds, according to a new State Department report. In its annual global survey of terrorism the report says about 14,000 attacks took place in 2006, mainly in Iraq and Afghanistan. These strikes claimed more than 20,000 lives, two-thirds in Iraq. That is 3,000 more attacks than in 2005 and 5,800 more deaths.[33]

In modern times 9/11 forms a benchmark. The terrorist attacks on the Twin Towers in New York and the Pentagon in Washington as well as the crash of the fourth airliner in Pennsylvania killed almost three thousand people.

October 2002 saw the murder of 202 vacationers in the seaside haven of Bali in Indonesia. The murders were perpetrated by the radical Jemmah Islamiah terrorist organization. Officials in the United States and Australia contended that Abu Bashir Baka, the spiritual leader of Jemmiah Islamiah, had a direct role in the bombings of the Bali nightclubs and of the bombing of the Marriott Hotel in Jakarta that killed twelve people in August 2003. Although sentenced to only thirty months in prison after a court found him guilty of a "sinister conspiracy" in connection with the bombings, he was released after one year because he was given credit for previous time served and for good behavior.

In March 2004, just days before Spain's elections, the city of Madrid was brought to a standstill as a result of a terrorist bombing of the metropolitan train line that killed 190 people. Again, Al Qaeda claimed responsibility for the attacks.

Later that year in September, Chechnyan terrorists surrounded a primary school in Beslan, a small town in Russia. As a result of the siege 334 civilians were killed including 186 children. Hundreds more were wounded. The attack was particularly chilling because the killings were broadcast by the international media as they were happening.

In July 2005, London was rocked by four suicide attacks that left fifty-four people dead and 345 wounded. The attacks involved the placing of bombs in the London subway and on a bus in Trafalgar Square. Within days Al Qaeda claimed responsibility for the atrocities promising further attacks.

In India, Sri Lanka, and Pakistan between 2002 and 2007 there were more than five hundred suicide attacks. The most high profile victim of these attacks was Benazir Bhutto, who was murdered while riding in a motorcade in December 2007.

Geography has no relevance to terrorism. In 2004 the Australian Government Department of Foreign Affairs and Trade issued a paper outlining the relevance of terrorism to Australia. The report commented:

"For the first time, Australians are having to come to terms with a security threat neither constrained nor defined by national borders, traditional power structures or formed armies—one that is neither dependent on sponsoring nation states, nor responsive to traditional deterrence. Rather, it is driven by an ideology that is inaccessible to reason, and with objectives that cannot be negotiated."[34]

Quite apart from the direct and collateral damage that has been inflicted on civilians around the world, terrorism is also responsible for the creation of an atmosphere of uncertainty and instability as government leaders continue to argue that a mega-terrorist attack is no longer a question of if but when. Ironically and tragically, the uncertainty created by the terrorist threat creates the very vulnerability required for recruitment to its cause. It is a frightening reality.

Cults, Terror, and the Internet

"According to Japanese newspaper reports, when the Tokyo police examined a number of CD Roms confiscated from a building owned by the Aum Shinri Kyo cult, they found huge email address lists of Japanese college students. The authorities believe that the cult may have sent out more than 40,000 emails in an attempt to recruit college students."[35]

"From websites spewing vitriolic messages of hate and recruiting the young to join in the sponsor's organizations, to technology attacks, to the consummation of terrorist conspiracies through e-mail, bulletin boards, extranets and downloadable files with target coordinates and recipes for bombs, the Internet has become a potent tool for the spread of hate and violence. Instead of standing on a street corner and handing out mimeographed leaflets, hate mongers may now promote their causes at sites on the World Wide Web and in chat rooms. The Internet facilitates communication among like-minded bigots across borders and oceans and enhances their ability to promote and recruit for their causes anonymously and cheaply."[36]

A significant development in the cult and terrorism arena has been the ability to utilize the Internet to broadcast messages on a global scale. Young people, teenagers, and adolescents can connect with cults at the press of a button.[37] Advances in the field of information technology have assisted smaller, less affluent groups in advancing their causes. While thirty years ago cults required a structure and some form of organizational identity to spread their word and promote their cause, today, with little more than a modem and a PC, a small group or single operator can access a world market.

In the 1960s and 1970s shopping malls and transport terminals were the recruiting grounds for many cults and alternative religious groups. Today, the grounds for recruitment have shifted as the Internet becomes an ever-increasing force and source of information.

Dr. Michael Carr-Gregg, from the Center of Adolescent Health in Melbourne, Australia, writes, "Of course, our children don't need to leave home to be seduced; the Internet is replete with a variety of spiritual predators, using chat sites to spread their gospel and glossy graphics to lure new members."[38]

Larry Trachte, a professor at Wartburg College in Iowa, says, "The Internet puts them in touch; instead of standing at airports, suddenly (the cults) have contacts with millions of people."[39]

The capacity for the Internet as a tool for recruitment was highlighted by a research study aimed at determining the kinds of psychological features people have when they are overly involved in usage of the Internet. The research centered on a sample of Internet users who had been diagnosed as Internet addicts. Significantly, this group "reported the highest degree of loneliness, depressed mood, and compulsivity compared to the other groups. This group seemed to be more vulnerable to interpersonal dangers than others, showing an unusually close feeling for strangers."[40]

Terrorist organizations are able to rely on the Internet as an invaluable and effective tool to spread their message. Radical Islamist websites preach terror and horror with very few controls available to curtail their spread of this social poison. The websites serve as powerful recruitment tools drawing in disaffected and marginalized youth to join the ranks of the borgeoning organizations.

According to Gabriel Weimann of the University of Haifa, in 2006 there were about five thousand terrorist websites that featured recruitment, training, sharing ideology, communication, and propaganda. Weimann comments that terrorist sites operate on three planes. The first one is the claim that the terrorists have no choice other than to turn to violence. "Violence is presented as a necessity foisted upon the weak as the only means with which to respond to an oppressive enemy. The terrorist organization is depicted as constantly persecuted, its leaders subject to assassination attempts and its supporters massacred, its freedom of expression curtailed, and its adherents arrested. This tactic, which portrays the organization as small, weak, and hunted down by a strong power or a strong state, turns the terrorists into the underdog."[41]

The second plane is targeted at justifying the use of violence by demonizing and delegitimizing the enemy. Members of the movement or organization are presented as freedom fighters, forced against their will to use violence because a ruthless enemy is crushing the rights and dignity of their people or group. The enemy of the movement or the organization is the real terrorist, many sites insist. "Our violence is tiny in comparison to his aggression" is a common argument. Terrorist rhetoric tries to shift the responsibility for violence from the terrorist to the adversary who is accused of displaying brutality, inhumanity, and immorality.

The third plane is the extensive use of the language of nonviolence in an attempt to counter the terrorists' violent image. Although these are violent organizations, many of their sites claim that they seek peaceful solutions, that their ultimate aim is a diplomatic settlement achieved through negotiation and international pressure on a repressive government.

The Internet enables terrorist organizations to not only solicit donations from sympathizers but also to recruit and mobilize supporters to play a more active role in support of terrorist activities or causes. Even though most of these websites appear to stop short of enlisting recruits for violent action, they do encourage their supporters to show their commitment to the cause in tangible ways.

In addition to seeking converts by using the full panoply of website technologies to enhance the presentation of their message, terrorist organizations capture information about the users who browse their websites. Users who seem most interested in the organization's cause or who are well suited to carrying out its work are then contacted. Recruiters may also use more interactive Internet technology to roam online chat rooms and cybercafés, looking for receptive members of the public, particularly young people. Electronic bulletin boards and user nets—issue-specific chat rooms and bulletin boards—can also serve as vehicles for reaching out to potential recruits.

Some would-be recruits, it may be noted, use the Internet to advertise themselves to terrorist organizations. In 1995 Ziyad Khalil enrolled as a computer science major at Columbia College in Missouri. He also became a Muslim activist on the campus, developing links to several radical groups and operating a website that supported Hamas. Thanks in large part to his Internet activities, he came to the attention of Osama bin Laden and his lieutenants. Khalil became Al Qaeda's procurement officer in the United States, arranging purchases of satellite telephones, computers, and other electronic surveillance technologies and helping bin Laden communicate with his followers and officers.[42]

Weimann argues that more typically terrorist organizations go looking for recruits rather than waiting for them to present themselves. The SITE Institute, a Washington-based terrorism research group that monitors Al Qaeda's Internet communications, has provided chilling details of a high-tech recruitment drive launched in 2003 to recruit fighters to travel to Iraq and attack U.S. and coalition forces there. Potential recruits are bombarded with religious decrees and anti-American propaganda, provided with training manuals on how to be a terrorist, and, as they are led through a maze of secret chat rooms, given specific instructions on how to make the journey to Iraq.[43]

Significantly, however, while the Internet may have become an invaluable tool for cult and terrorist organizations, it also serves as a means for the public to learn about them. Websites set up by former members of cults as well as sites that feature research information on particular suspect political organizations can assist people to understand more about these groups and their agendas.[44]

In an unusual use of the Internet, in January 2008 a notorious group known as Anonymous disabled a Scientology website after declaring war on the church. In a message posted on YouTube, the group said it was tired of the methods used by the church to stem criticism of Scientology. Critics say that the church is famous for vigorously attacking its critics, often taking legal action or attempting to undermine their credibility.

"Anonymous has therefore decided your organization should be destroyed, for the good of your followers, for the good of mankind and for our own enjoyment," a synthesized voice said in the clip. "We shall systematically expel you from the Internet and proceed to dismantle the Church of Scientology in its current form."[45]

It can be safely assumed that the Internet will continue to be used by cult and terrorist organizations as well by those who attempt to expose the hidden agendas, goals, and objectives of these organizations. Clearly, the Internet is becoming an increasingly important force in the battle for people's minds and lives.

Heralding passage of the Cyber Security Enhancement Act in 2002, a Republican congressman from Texas, Lamar Smith, stated, "Until we secure our cyber infrastructure, a few keystrokes and an Internet connection are all one needs to disable the economy and endanger lives. A mouse can be just as dangerous as a bullet or a bomb."[46]

2

Understanding Mind Control

everal years ago I traveled to California to talk to a woman who had become entangled with a faith healer. Her family had become alarmed when she approached her two teenage daughters with a plea that they offer themselves as sexual brides to her healer who claimed that he required these liaisons in order to restore his own health. The woman was a career professional who had worked as a CEO in a multi-national company. Friends described her as a model mother who raised her children with impeccable morals.

On another occasion I was asked to prepare a professional report to assist a young woman who had been charged with loitering and prostitution. She had been a member of the Children of God. In search of new members, she had offered her services to an undercover policeman. The woman had been the top student in her school. Her valedictory speech was titled "In Search of Morality." Prior to joining the cult she had received an award for outstanding contributions in the field of youth and outreach work.

I also met with an Australian family whose daughter had become involved in a terrorist youth organization in Afghanistan. Her communication with the family had become quite infrequent, and eventually the family lost contact with her altogether. As I write this, it has been four years since they have heard from her, and they have no idea if she is alive.

The London bombings of July 2005 created shockwaves across the world as the phenomenon of the home-grown terrorist became a reality. Murderers had kissed their wives and children goodbye as they set off on their final mission of destruction. The attacks emphasized that there was no clear profile of a terrorist. According to the British Home Office, the four attackers had come from relatively comfortable homes, and there was little in their backgrounds that marked them as particularly vulnerable to radicalization. Their bombs were constructed from readily available materials and required little expertise.[47]

What is mind control and how does it work? Were the victims of Jonestown, Waco, Heaven's Gate, or the Order of the Solar Temple programmed to their deaths, or did they have any rational role in what happened to them? Can terrorists absolve themselves from responsibility for their actions on the basis that they were brainwashed?

Does the phenomenon of mind control absolve the perpetrator of responsibility for their execution of terrorist acts and other horrific crimes? Is mind control an effective defense in court?

And what about the children who have been reared in cultures ridden with hatred and prejudice and who have had the destructive idea of martyrdom implanted in their minds before they developed the mental capacity to digest this information?

If, in fact, people can have their minds controlled, is there an effective means by which this process can be reversed? And what about civil libertarians who feel that any attempt to alter the thinking patterns of a cult or terrorist member is a gross invasion of that individual's rights?

An increasing body of evidence supports the view that under the right conditions peace-loving altruistic young men and women can be turned into killers or terrorists. If proven true, this is an extremely frightening thesis.

What Is Mind Control? Does It Exist?

"I am convinced, based on more than three decades of studying New Religious Movements, through participant-observation and through interviews with both members and ex-members, that these movements

*have unleashed social and psychological forces of truly awesome power.
These forces have wreaked havoc in many lives—in both adults and
in children. It is these social and psychological influence processes that
the social scientist has both the right and the duty to try to understand,
regardless of whether such understanding will ultimately prove helpful
or harmful to the cause of religious liberty.*[48]

Mind control is the process by which individual or collective freedom of choice and action is compromised by agents or agencies
that modify or distort perception, motivation, affect, cognition, and
behavior. It is neither magical nor mystical but a process that involves a set of basic, social psychological principles.[49]

According to Philip Zimbardo, professor emeritus of psychology
at Stanford University and a founder of the National Center for the
Psychology of Terrorism, "conformity, compliance, persuasion, disso-
nance, reactance, guilt and fear arousal, modeling, and identification
are some of the staple social influence ingredients well studied in
psychological experiments and field studies. In some combinations
they create a powerful crucible of extreme mental and behavioral manipulation with several other real-world factors such as charismatic,
authoritarian leaders, dominant ideologies, social isolation, physical
debilitation, induced phobias, and extreme threats or promised rewards that are typically deceptively orchestrated over an extended
time period in settings where they are applied intensively."

Zimbardo argues that a body of social science evidence shows
that when systematically practiced by state-sanctioned police, military, or destructive cults, mind control can induce false confessions,
create converts who willingly torture or kill "invented enemies," engage indoctrinated members to work tirelessly, give up their money,
and even their lives for the cause.[50]

In society there are numerous elaborate methods to influence attitudes and modify behavior. However, thought reform programs can
be distinguished from other social influence efforts because of their
totalistic views and their use of sequenced phases aimed at destabi-

lizing a participant's sense of self, reality, and values. According to Margaret Singer, "Thought reform programs rely on organized peer pressure, the development of bonds between the leader or trainer and the followers, the control of communication, and the use of a variety of influence techniques. The aim of all this is to promote conformity, compliance, and the adoption of specific attitudes and behaviors desired by the group."[51]

Thought reform is facilitated through the use of psychological and environmental control processes that do not depend on physical coercion. Thought reform programs are sophisticated, subtle, and insidious, creating a psychological bond that in many ways is far more powerful than gun-at-the-head methods of influence.

In response to arguments rejecting mind control or thought reform as a psychological phenomenon, Singer points to the inclusion of thought reform in the *Diagnostic and Statistical Manual of Mental Disorders* (DSM-IV) as evidence that this orchestrated process of exploitative psychological manipulation is real and recognized within the professional psychiatric field. "To say then that the concept of thought reform is rejected by the scientific community is false and irresponsible. The phenomenon has been studied and discussed since 1951, and continuing studies by social psychologists and other behavioral scientists have solidified our understandings of its components and overall impact."[52]

Significantly, this view is supported by a research paper produced by the Rand Corporation on recruitment methods used by Al Qaeda. Titled "Terrorist Selection and Recruitment," the paper argues that terrorist organizations create physical and mental trauma to produce a dissociative state in the target individual—a condition in which identity, memory, consciousness and awareness and rational thought are in flux. Coupled with that dissociation is the creation of a new identity and new thought processes—a transformation—along the lines sought by the recruiter.[53]

Although the paper acknowledges that not every recruit to Al Qaeda is brainwashed or coerced, it argues that "many techniques used in classic, predatory thought reform are used by Al Qaeda." Moreover, most of the techniques used by predatory totalist groups such as cults are shared by Al Qaeda. Indeed, the Rand Corporation report argues that Al Qaeda is a totalist group because it seeks to completely transform and dominate the lives of its members with more powerful tools than those used by Aum Shinri Kyo, the People's Church, or the Chinese "thought reform" of American POWs in the Korean war.[54]

In support of the argument that terrorists are brainwashed, a report published in 2002 by the Dutch intelligence service found that Al Qaeda had "explicitly instructed" recruiters to base themselves in Europe and troll for aspiring jihadis in prisons, mosques, and other gathering places. Recruiters used psychological techniques such as isolating recruits and assigning them a buddy to serve as a continuous source of influence, according to a report by the intelligence service.[55]

There are dissenting views. Marc Sageman, a senior fellow at the Foreign Policy Research Institute in Philadelphia, rejects the mind control argument. Sageman claims that, "Joining the Jihad is more akin to the process of applying to a selective college. Many try to get in, but only a few succeed, and the college's role is evaluation and selection rather than marketing."[56]

David Canter, a psychology professor at the University of Liverpool and the Director of the Center of Investigative Psychology, argues that terrorists, even suicide bombers, are neither mad, nor psychopaths, nor brainwashed. Canter claims that the fact that some of the terrorists interviewed by his colleagues in India could argue very logically and coherently proved that they weren't brainwashed.[57] This view is contradicted by other researchers who argue that the ability of people to think logically cannot be used as proof that they are not brainwashed. Some terrorists and, for that matter, cult members function quite well.

While many professionals have provided explanations of mind control, Robert J. Lifton's list of eight definitive characteristics provides one of the best introductions to this complex process.

Eight Characteristics of Mind Control

According to Lifton, a professor of psychology and psychiatry at John Jay College and the Graduate Center of the City University of New York, cults can be identified by three characteristics: one, a charismatic leader who increasingly becomes an object of worship as the general principles that may have sustained the group lose power; two, a process of coercive persuasion or thought reform; three, economic, sexual, and other forms of exploitation of group members by the leader.[58]

Lifton studied Chinese thought reform methods as well as the psychology of Nazi doctors. In doing so he arrived at a list of eight definitive characteristics of cult organizations that have since become a mental health standard. He suggested that the best way to determine whether a particular group is destructive is to compare its behavior and conduct with these eight criteria.[59]

1. Milieu Control

Milieu control refers to total control of communication in a group. Gossip or expressions of doubt about the group are forbidden. Members are directed to report peers who break rules, to limit or eliminate contact with relatives, and to ignore media reports.

> "Members of the Exclusive Brethren are restricted from using television, radios, computers, record and CD players. A leader of the group in New Zealand says 'We don't like using the airwaves normally. Satan is the prince of the power of the air and that medium is used to get right into a believer's home. We don't want that.'"[60]

> "Once the suitable suicide candidate is selected, the person undergoes a lengthy preparation period, lasting three weeks to three months. During this period, the chosen person is often cocooned by the group and protected from outside influences, particularly the candidate's family, television and radio. In confinement, the

candidate is immersed in the teachings of the Koran and repeatedly told the suicide attack will put that person in favor with God."[61]

2. Loading of the Language

Cults typically impose a language that is unique to the group. The continual use of chosen clichés and expressions creates a sense of camaraderie that unites members and sets them apart from a world sometimes described as satanic, evil, or unclean.

"A prime hurdle for former cult members is to overcome speaking and thinking in the cult's special language. As we have seen, each group has its own jargon, usually based on applying new and idiosyncratic meanings to regular words and phrases. The jargon creates a sense of eliteness, solidarity, and belonging among those in the in-group; at the same time, it cuts people off from easy conversation with outsiders. This is true even in the live-out cults, whose members work at outside jobs but put in most of their free time with the cult; during that time with the cult, they speak the group jargon. In certain groups, the loaded language is more centrally encompassing than in others and thus harder to shed afterward."[62]

"Juan Cole, President of the Global Americana Institute, argues that the ability of the September 11 terrorists to carry out their mission was influenced by an almost obsessive-compulsive immersion in the details of repeated rituals. He says that every activity involved in the preparation of the attacks was accompanied by the uttering of specific phrases. The constant hum of this recitation may have been intended to induce a liminal state that was not entirely conscious."[63]

3. A Demand for Purity

Cults create a radical separation of good and evil. The cult is right; the world is wrong. Acts are either good or bad, and people are viewed in black-and-white terms. The appeal to purity allows the cult to let ends justify means. Deception and lying are acceptable because they serve the pure aim of the cult.

Apocalyptic cults spread the message that individuals are either members of the group and will, therefore, survive, or they are not and are doomed. In order to draw people into the group and save them, members can lie, because those who are saved will ultimately appreciate these actions.

> "Shoko Asahara, the charismatic leader of the Aum Shinri Kyo cult, predicted an apocalypse that only cult members would survive.[64]
>
> Luc Juret, leader of the Order of the Solar Temple, like many cult leaders, told his followers of a coming apocalypse. He explained this would occur through environmental disasters and only the elect would survive.[65]
>
> *Scott* Caruthers, leader of an obscure group known as the BDX cult, preached that members of his cult would survive the apocalypse and everyone else on earth would be destroyed."[66]
>
> "Terrorists tend to have an apocalyptic and somewhat simplified worldview in which good is pitted against evil and in which their adversaries are to blame for their woes. They believe that through their actions, they can uphold their values of family, religion, ethnicity, and nationality and bring about the triumph of the good. Acting on God's behalf to defend these values is viewed as more important than life."[67]

4. Confession

Cults encourage members to admit everything about their past and present behavior. Although the member is told that the confession will set him free, in effect it binds him to the group since the confessed information can be used against him. Furthermore, leaving the cult becomes more difficult, as the member feels that he will have left behind an intimate part of himself.

Some personal development groups, such as Money & You, an

organization operating in Australia, involve activities in which individuals are encouraged to share their innermost feelings with other participants. Such sharing reinforces allegiance to the group. Confessions are often made very publicly so that group members are privy to very personal and often intimate information about their peers.

> "Common routines in MKO, the Mojahedin-e Khalq terrorist organization, include self criticizing and confession sessions. The members have to write detailed daily reports of activities, their previous night's dreams, their thoughts, and even love and emotional daydreams. In some cases, they are forced to read their reports before other members and suffer humiliation. Ali Qachqaoui, a separated member, reveals: "They remote controlled us, like robots. They told us, 'If you have sexual fantasies, even a dream, you must report it in writing in order to exorcise it.'"[68]

5. Mystical Manipulation

The process of mystical manipulation or planned spontaneity is designed to make members feel they have chosen to belong to the group and that their allegiance to the cult is a totally voluntary act. Events in the cult are planned to look spontaneous, when, in fact, they are carefully orchestrated by the leadership.

> "According to Erica Heftman, a former member of the Moonies and author of the book, Behind the Darker Side of the Moonies, there were jokes which were told every day, there were stories which were made to sound spontaneous, but everything was planned beforehand."[69]
>
> "At the 2008 hearing of Ali Hamza Ahmad Suliman al-Bahlul on charges to commit murder and terrorism, Bahlul renounced his Yemeni citizenship because Yemen was cooperating with the United States and had thus sworn allegiance to the enemy. He renewed his allegiance to Osama bin Laden. 'Today I say to you that I will never deny that I have participated with Osama bin Laden

in fighting you because I'm looking for a greater day than today,' he said. 'I am responsible for my actions in this world and in the next world, meaning I don't care if you imprison me or kill me.'"[70]

6. Doctrine over Person

Cults encourage members to interpret reality through their doctrine and to ignore personal experiences that conflict with the group's beliefs. If the member's experience is at odds with the cult dogma, the experience is to be disregarded. Contradictions become associated with guilt; doubt indicates one's own deficiency or evil.

"Bhagwan Rajneesh, the former guru of a group known as the Orange People, wrote in his newsletter, 'The Master first has to destroy all your beliefs, theist, atheist, Catholic, communist; the Master has to dismantle all your structures of belief, so that you are left again as a small child, innocent, open, ready to inquire, ready to plunge into the adventures of truth.'"[71]

"No wonder Farhad agreed to go to Jalalabad to kill a fellow Muslim. Still, wasn't there a doubt in his mind about taking his life like that and who knows how many others? No. The Taliban had told him that when he pushed the button on his suicide vest, it was Allah then who would decide whether to summon him to heaven or not."[72]

7. Sacred Science

The term *sacred science* is used to describe the cult leader's claim to wisdom and the further claim that his philosophy is relevant to all humankind. Anyone who disagrees is not only immoral but unscientific.

"American-born Franklin Jones, now known by his devotees as Adi Da, the Da Avatar, writes, 'I am the inherent being. I am the perfectly subjective truth of the world, made incarnate, plain, and obvious as man, and to man. I am the life and consciousness of all beings.'"[73]

"In one of bin Laden's videos released after the events of September 11, it is clear that the terrorist leader is patterning his life after the Prophet Muhammad, and feels himself blessed with the same degree of divine approval for his violent struggle with the enemies of God. His perverse success in persuading thousands of young Muslim men to fight and die for him is very likely due to their perception of him as a Muhammad figure—an inspiring warrior-prophet who embodies the wrathful power of Allah."[74]

8. Dispensing of Existence

Cults often teach that those who have not seen the light are wedded to evil, tainted, and, therefore, lack the right even to exist. Hence, a cult member threatened with being cast out of the group may experience a fear of extinction or collapse. This is the final step in creating a member's dependence on the group.

Former members of a Christian fundamentalist group sought assistance from our organization claiming their minds had been raped and their material possessions stolen. When asked why it had taken several years for them to seek help they responded by explaining that even now they feared this action would forever deny them the opportunity for salvation.

"The Taliban's name for its secret police is Ministry of Enforcement of Virtue and Suppression of Vice. The terrorist organization sees the world in terms of an epic battle between good and evil. There is a strong narcissist component in many of the leaders of terrorist groups. By definition, narcissism means an excessive feeling of love for oneself, giving more value to oneself over someone else. The thinking is, 'I can use other people and then get rid of them, as if they were an empty milk carton.'"[75]

Not every cult or terrorist group will demonstrate all eight of the above characteristics, and organizations that appear to exercise undue control over their followers need to be assessed individually.

Similarly, not everyone who expresses interest in a particular cult or terrorist organization will become indoctrinated as a member.

And even for those who do establish connections to these organizations, their level of attachment, the control exercised by the leadership, and their relationship to the group's dynamics will depend on a range of factors. There are some individuals whose involvement in established mainstream religion is very cult-like. Then there are others, who may frequent a fringe church, ashram, or even a terrorist organization, but remain free from any of the symptoms of mind control or undue subjugation to the leader of the group.

In a similar manner, individuals may be attracted to some of the social service networks offered by terrorist organizations and refrain altogether from becoming involved in any acts of violence. They are not necessarily victims of mind control.

Nevertheless, the issue remains contentious. Writing in *Slate* magazine regarding the brainwashing defense being used in cult- and terrorist-related matters, columnist Dahlia Lithwick argues, "If anyone has been brainwashed, it's the millions of Americans who still view new, radicalized, or unusual religions as 'cults' and their leaders as masters of mind control. We must try these terror cases free from the patronizing assumption that strange, even crazy beliefs are necessarily products of illness or undue influence. The proper word to describe a savage act committed at the behest of a charismatic lunatic is not 'brainwashed.' It's evil." [76]

Control of Behavior, Thoughts, Emotions, Information, and the Environment

In his epic work *Combating Mind Control*, Steve Hassan has identified four components of mind control: control of behavior, control of thoughts, control of emotions, and control of information. I believe that control of the environment is also significant.

Behavior Control

Inside a cult organization behavior control is exercised in the regulation of an individual's physical reality—where he lives, what clothing he wears, what food he eats, how much sleep he gets, as well as the jobs, rituals, and other actions he performs.

Fasting, strict diet, the wearing of particular clothes, as well as highly regulated timetables, can be elements of behavior control, leaving members with little or no private time. Reward and punishment codes further restrict individual freedom as compliance takes on new significance. The regulation of a member's personal budget will mean that he no longer has control over his finances and thus must resort to borrowing from the cult. Such loans in turn create further dependence on and attachment to the cult.

Terrorist organizations control behavior by discouraging individuality, encouraging "groupthink," imposing rigid rules, and enforcing obedience. The collective identity of terrorists is established extremely early, so that hatred is deeply internalized. The importance of collective identities and the processes of forming and transforming them cannot be overemphasized. Terrorists subordinate their individual identity to the collective identity, so that what serves the group, organization, or network is of primary importance.

"She lived in, and created for us, a world of deceptions, lies and inconsistencies…. By her control over the spiritual aspects of our lives, by her subjugation of us by physical means, and by her constant assault on our belief in our own worth, Anne Hamilton-Byrne was able to systematically break down our sense of self."[77]

"Within the terrorist framework, you almost invariably get an authoritarian leadership and organization; a regimentation of members. The leader and followers 'insist on absolute conformity —not only conformity of action but of thought and feelings.'"[78]

Thought Control

Successful cults indoctrinate their members so thoroughly that individuals internalize the group doctrine, incorporate a new language, and are taught to keep their mind centered. In order to be a good member, a person must learn to manipulate his thought processes.

Cult members are discouraged from thinking negatively about the cult and often given thought-stopping techniques to be used mechanically in the face of negative thoughts. Singing, chanting, speaking in tongues, humming, and focusing on the guru may be used in response to doubt, anxiety, and stress.

Particular expressions, clichés, sentences are also vehicles for thought control. In the same way as a new student looks forward to mastering the language of his course, so too does the cult member regard the mastering of the group's language as a goal.

"Often cult members agree to talk to exit counselors only because of extreme pressure from family members. In such cases, cult members may resist the efforts of the exit counselors by praying, chanting, or using some other thought stopping technique that the cult has taught them to use in such circumstances. This is usually something that the family alone is totally unprepared for and this is when a trained, professional exit counselor becomes essential."[79]

"Candidates who enlist as suicide bombers are expected to immerse themselves in spiritual contemplation and prayer, to free their minds of negative thoughts toward their fellow men—except Americans and their Iraqi 'infidel' supporters. There is no TV, music or cigarettes. In many ways, these steps mirror the self-purification that devout Muslims undergo before embarking on the pilgrimage to Mecca. 'You give up your previous life and start a new one.'"[80]

Emotional Control

In a cult setting various forms of emotional control are used to manipulate and narrow the range of a person's feelings. Guilt and fear are necessary tools to keep people under control.

Hassan points out that cults often create the image of a persecuting enemy. This enemy can take the form of authority, such as the FBI involvement with the Branch Davidians at Waco. Jim Jones was convinced that he was being targeted by the U.S. government. Exit counselors are also the enemy. Some groups go to extraordinary lengths in order to denigrate exit counselors and anti-cult organizations.

The creation of phobias or phobia indoctrination is a powerful technique of emotional control. Members may be warned that if they leave the cult they will experience disaster, get killed in a plane crash, or die prematurely.

The creation of phobias may lead to severe panic attacks at the thought of leaving. Eventually, it does not matter that the members can leave at any time. The doors can be left wide open. After her capture by the police, Patty Hearst acknowledged that she had the freedom to escape from the Symbionese Liberation Army but had not taken that option.

One of my first clients was a woman who had been thrown out of a cult some eight years before she saw me. She had since married but was afraid of becoming pregnant, as she had been told that her children would be stillborn. She eventually did become pregnant and miscarried after three months. Her doctor suggested that her deep-seated fears and constant anxiety contributed to the miscarriage.

"Some cults inculcate their followers with notions that they will get sick, fall from grace, lose energy or somehow suffer if they leave. Former members may worry indefinitely about their cult leader's dire predictions of the horrible events that will befall them and their families. Because they have been so well trained, former cult members may continue to see this possible fate as something they may bring on themselves by having left the group, given up on their faith, and betrayed the cause."[81]

"The simple reason is the terrifying brainwashing suffered by most of the Arab youth at the hands of 'religious clerics' and particularly at the hands of the extremists with backward views. These 'clerics' nourish the Muslim youth with various kinds of racist views and destructive extremist principles, and nurse them with hostility, hatred, and resentment towards other people and towards members of other divine religions."[82]

Information Control

Comparable to milieu control in Lifton's model, information control refers to the practice of withholding information not conducive to cult adherence as well as the selective presentation of other forms of information.

Many groups deny their members access to television or other forms of the media. They may provide a buddy to ensure that there is some control when outside family members visit. If information is passed on during that time that contradicts the cult's ideology, every effort will be made to neutralize that effect. It is not uncommon for cults to screen both incoming and outgoing mail.

Negative media reports about the cult and its leadership are withheld. In the event of information leaking into the cult, there are damage control mechanisms. The media is Satan's agent, and the information disseminated is labeled a test.

"In November 2007, a handful of doomsday cult members on Friday crawled out of the damp cave in the Penza region where they spent six months waiting for the end of the world, which their leader had prophesied. Pyotr Kuznetsov, who declared himself a prophet several years earlier, and was subsequently admitted to a psychiatric hospital, reportedly told followers that in the afterlife they would be judging whether others deserved heaven or hell. Followers were not allowed to watch television, listen to the radio or handle money."[83]

"Within terrorist organizations, the media is significant in this area in a number of ways. Firstly, some media - —nate propaganda which contributes to violent radicalization. Typically this conveys a reductionist and conspiratorial worldview where inequity and oppression are dominant and entire countries, religions or societies are depicted in a way which denies them human dignity and presents them as collectively guilty."[84]

Control of the Environment

The phenomona of terror and suicide bombing reveal another aspect of cultism that needs to be considered to understand the process of indoctrination. Pedahzur writes: "In order for suicide terrorism to be a viable alternative, there must be a culture that supports, even glorifies, death, a sense of supreme hopelessness and an asymmetrical alignment of forces where a small group is confronting a much larger and more powerful force."[85]

In a community that either is or perceives itself to be oppressed by external powers and where an improvement in its situation seems impossible, dying in a suicide attack may be regarded as an honorable way to help one's community while ensuring eternal salvation.

> "The compound of the Fundamental Church of Jesus Christ of Latter Day Saints, known as 'The Yearning for Zion Ranch,' is situated 5 miles off the highway. It is as self-sufficient as it is isolated, with a cheese-making plant, a cement plant, orchards, gardens, a doctor's office and a school. The use of the internet is forbidden. Television, newspapers and magazines are prohibited. There is a purpose to being cut off from the world. Members believe the apocalypse is near and they will have to start over when the world is destroyed."[86]

"The goal is satisfying Allah and his instructions. No money interests, nothing. No brainwash, no pressure; it is my decision. All the other lies are pathetic propaganda. I pray that Allah gives me the honor to be dead in an operation. This is the supreme and the noblest way to ascend to Allah. These martyrs have special status in the next world and have bigger chances to watch Allah's face and enjoy the magnificent pleasures he offers us."[87]

Hassan comments that the four components of a cult—control of behavior, control of thoughts, control of emotions, and control of information—are guidelines. They are not necessarily all present in every cult or terrorist group. "What matters most is the overall impact on a person's free will and ability to make real choices. A person's uniqueness, talents, skills, creativity, and free will should be encouraged, not suppressed. Destructive mind control seeks to 'make people over' in the image of the cult leader. This process has been described as 'cloning'. This 'cult identity' is the result of a systematic process to dissociate a person from his or her previous identity including important beliefs and values as well as significant relationships."[88]

Whether in relation to cult indoctrination or the radicalization of terrorist recruits, these methods are powerful. Radical changes in the personalities of cult followers and terrorists only confirm the far-reaching nature of these methods.

Unfreezing, Changing, and Refreezing

In his book *Recovery from Cults*, Michael Langone provides a succinct account of the indoctrination process and explains how the methods described above work to change the personality of the recruit.

"Those who do make the commitment to join are rarely aware of the subtle techniques of persuasion and control influencing their behavior, thoughts and feelings. The apparent loving unanimity of the organization masks, and in some cases bolsters, strict rules against private as well as public dissent. Individuals may be told things like, 'you're intellectualizing,' or 'you're being divisive.' Doubt and dissent are thus interpreted as symptoms of personal deficiency."[89]

Once the dominance of the organization is established—once it is permanently one up—members or recruits slide down a spiral of increasing dependence. Members are often encouraged or ordered to live with other group members. People outside the organization are viewed as spiritually, psychologically, politically, or socially inferior, or as impediments to a member's development. Members are taught that in order to "advance" they must avoid outsiders and spend long hours involved in the various tasks or practices the leadership deems necessary.

To ensure continuation of the organization's rewards—which include praise, attention, the promise of future benefits, and social contact—members or recruits must implicitly, if not explicitly, acknowledge the organization's authority in defining what is real, good, and true.

Cult organizations challenge and test their members by establishing extremely high, if not impossible, expectations that may include fundraising quotas and personal development goals. Because dissent, doubt, and negativity are forbidden, members must project a façade of happiness and acceptance while struggling to achieve the impossible. Those who fail to establish the requisite façade are attacked and punished.

The result of this process, when carried to its conclusion, is a pseudo-personality, a state of dissociation in which members or recruits proclaim great happiness yet hide great suffering.[90]

Hassan refers to the notion of dual identity and suggests that despite all of the forces of mind control, the essential identity of the member or the recruit is never totally destroyed. Its presence and manifestation will depend on the level of indoctrination or psychological manipulation experienced. Families should not be misled by the apparent re-emergence of the old personality or a temporary return to the pre-cult presentation.

Lifton refers to this dramatic change of identity as doubling, "the formation of a second self which lives side by side with the former one, often for a considerable time."[91]

The manner by which cults or terrorist organizations actually change the behavior of potential adherents is described by Edgar Schein in a book called *Coercive Persuasion*. He posits three stages in this process that he calls as unfreezing, changing, and refreezing—a model based on the work of Kurt Lewin.[92] Schein describes unfreezing as breaking a person down, changing as the actual process of indoctrination, and refreezing as the rebuilding of a new identity or the pseudo-personality of the member or recruit.

Unfreezing includes the use of hypnosis and the inducement of a trance state. Changes in diet, sleep deprivation, a new wardrobe, denial of access to the media and other external stimuli are powerful agents of change. So too are negative comments about the new member, the denigration of the member's earlier life and family connections, as well as comments about his or her spiritual inadequacy.

Changing refers to the superimposition of a new identity. Hassan explains that many of the techniques used in the freezing phase are extended during this phase. Hypnosis, repetition, and monotony further cement the member to the new order of the cult and to further reinforce the belief that inside is good and outside bad. The pressure is on to drop one's past and create the new person with a new truth.

During this period the group may make an outright effort to implant its ideology in the recruit's mind. There may be an intense one-on-one dialogue that further strengthens the new member's commitment. Normal barriers of privacy may be broken down as the member is encouraged to share intimate private beliefs and experiences. The peer pressure to conform and join with others may be overwhelming while individuality is lost in the totality of the group experience.

Finally, the process of refreezing involves the creation of a new identity and new purpose. The member establishes a new life through external changes—in dress or name or adapting to a particular language—and internal changes by subjugating decisions to a leader and rejecting previous relationships and life experiences.

Now a full-fledged member, he or she may be sent out to collect funds or recruit others. Moreover, the group responds by attaching a level of importance and stature to the new member who now knows, or at least is under the impression that he knows, what is happening on the inside. He or she may now in turn withhold that information from newer recruits.

The effects of mind control, whether on a member who has been indoctrinated into a cult, or the recruit who has been radicalized by a terrorist organization, are strikingly similar. Commenting on these organizations, Walter Laqueur writes in his book *No End to War: Terrorism in the Twenty-first Century*, "Some of these sects have induced their members to commit collective suicide. If it is possible to persuade hundreds of people to commit suicide, it stands to reason that it is possible with equal ease to make them engage in suicide terrorism."

Mind Control and Culpability

"It seems quite odd to me that the American people have immediately accepted the fact that one man can brainwash 900 human beings into mass suicide, but will not accept the fact that a ruthless group, the Symbionese Liberation Army, could brainwash a little girl by torture, degradation and confinement."[93]

Whether being the victim of mind control discharges a person from culpability for misdemeanors or crimes committed under these circumstances is a complex issue. Courts have been divided over this issue.

In the high-profile case of Patty Hearst, who was kidnapped by the Symbionese Liberation Army and eventually arrested in Los Angeles, the court rejected the brainwashing defense. Hearst was eventually pardoned by former President Clinton on his last day in office in 2001.

In Japan, in court cases against members of Aum Shinri Kyo for the 1995 sarin gas attack on the Tokyo subway system, mind control was rejected as a defense or even a mitigating factor in relation to sentencing.

The issue also was raised in the defense of Lee Boyd Malvo who together with John Allen Muhammad terrorized the streets of Washington in 2002, randomly killing ten people. Cult expert Paul Martin argued that the teenage defendant's background, which included parental abandonment, his lack of a father figure, and drifter lifestyle left him vulnerable to indoctrination, or brainwashing, by a strong male influence like John Allen Muhammad.

> "People who become indoctrinated can sometimes develop a pseudo personality. They can develop a new sense of identity, a pseudo identity. In my own experience they can change their moral values. People who normally don't lie or cheat or steal will lie or cheat or steal. Women who are not sexually promiscuous can become sexually promiscuous. People can start to engage in crime and people can kill when they are under that mindset."[94]

The court rejected the argument. Regarding the case, Robert Lifton commented, "A strong person, particularly an older person, can have an enormous influence on the shaping of mind and behavior of another person, but there is still the issue of responsibility."

However, the court reached a different decision in the case of Karen Rubidoux. She was accused of starving her baby son, Samuel, to death. She was ultimately found not guilty, while her husband, convicted for the child's murder in 2002, is now serving a life sentence. The mother's attorney, Joseph Krowski, offered the defense that Karen Rubidoux's behavior was coerced through cult brainwashing, and that she was victimized, abused, and ultimately controlled by an obscure religious sect led by her father-in-law, Roland Rubidoux, called "The Body."[95]

"There were two victims here, Karen and Samuel," Rubidoux's older sister told the press. After seven hours of deliberation the jury agreed with the defense and its witnesses, acquitting the "cult" mother of murder but finding her guilty of a misdemeanor assault and battery.

"Because a child died, it may be an unpopular verdict, but we felt Karen Rubidoux's intent was not to kill her baby," the jury foreman said. "I do believe she was psychologically held prisoner," and concluded, "she has suffered enough."

In a landmark case, U.S. courts also ruled that cults and other pseudo-religious groups can be prosecuted for brainwashing their followers. In Wollersheim v. Church of Scientology, a California court stated that church practices had been conducted in a coercive environment and so were not protected by religious freedom guarantees. Wollersheim was finally awarded $8 million in damages.[96]

According to media reports during the trial, experts testified that Scientology's "auditing" and "disconnect" constituted brainwashing and thought reform practices akin to those the Chinese and North Koreans had used on American prisoners of war. "Using its position as religious leader, the 'church' and its agents coerced Wollersheim into continuing auditing even though his sanity was repeatedly threatened by this practice. Thus there is adequate proof the religious practice in this instance caused real harm to the individual and the appellant's outrageous conduct caused that harm. 'Church' practices conducted in a coercive environment are not qualified to be voluntary religious practices entitled to first amendment religious freedom guarantees."[97]

In 1993 the European Court of Human Rights upheld the rights of a Greek Jehovah's Witness, Minos Kokkinakis, who had been sentenced to prison and a fine for proselytizing to spread his faith, though the court sought to define what it regarded as acceptable ways of sharing one's faith. However, in a dissenting judgment two judges argued that Kokkinakis and his wife had applied "unacceptable psychological techniques" akin to brainwashing.[98]

The alleged terrorist Zacarias Moussaoui was detained in New York on immigration law violations and may have been the twentieth hijacker in the 9/11 terror attacks on the World Trade Center and the Pentagon. He was arrested two weeks before the attacks. In seeking to mitigate his culpability, Moussaoui's brother, Abd Samad Moussaoui, said that Zacarias once loved America. Speaking in October 2001, Abd Samad said that his brother "once loved everything about America, including blue jeans and Bruce Springsteen. However, he came to hate the U.S. after joining a radical Islamic group in London that brainwashed him."[99]

John Phillip Walker Lindh pleaded guilty to providing services to the Taliban and carrying explosives. His parents and attorneys attempted to mount a defense that he was brainwashed by the Taliban. "John loves America," his father told reporters. "John did not take up arms against America. He never meant to harm any American, and he never did harm any American. John is innocent of these charges."[100]

This argument was also advanced by FACTnet, a group that exposes cults and mind control. "It does not make sense to Americans that John Walker Lindh should be found amongst the Taliban and, seemingly, willing to take up arms against fellow Americans; unless he is seen in the more probable and logical context that he is a victim of modern mind control and cult techniques."[101]

The connection between mind control and culpability is contentious, and courts continue to deliberate the issue. Significantly, in most of the cases where this issue has been relevant, the courts have recognized the argument that mind control can be an important factor in determining the outcome of a particular case. The question is still open whether mind control is sufficient to warrant acquittal of a crime.

3

The Subtle
Process of
Recruitment

Several months after the attacks of 9/11, I was touched by another event that grabbed international headlines. As a headline, the story faded very quickly; as an insight into the human psyche, it was far more significant.

In January 2002, a lonely and troubled fifteen-year-old American teenager managed to steal a Cessna aircraft from a St. Petersburg flying school and crash it into the twenty-eighth and twenty-ninth floors of the forty-two story Bank of America building in Tampa, Florida. Described by police as a deliberate copy of the attacks of 9/11, young Charles Bishop left a suicide note indicating he sympathized with Osama bin Laden. He sent no farewell message.

One expert said his suicide letter shows the delusional mindset of someone suffering depression, someone who felt insignificant and unappreciated. "He wasn't saying 'goodbye,'" said Donna Cohen, professor of psychiatry at the University of South Florida. "He was saying, 'I am.' He's angry." Significantly, Cohen said the letter showed that "in his loneliness and anger and feeling lost, he's found a cause, something to fill up his emptiness."[102]

In a June 2008 article titled "The Loneliness of the Child Suicide Bomber," journalist Kim Senputa wrote about the plight of Shakirullah Yassin Ali, a small frail boy, just fourteen, who was arrested as he prepared to carry out a suicide bombing against British and American targets in Afghanistan. When he was told by the mullahs that the time had come for him to serve God in Afghanistan, he requested to be allowed to see his parents. He was told it was not possible for security reasons but the family would be paid well for what he was doing.[103]

I believe that the issue of loneliness and the desperate need to belong is a far more pervasive issue than society would like to believe. The issue of loneliness lies at the heart of much perverse and destructive behavior. The link between pornography and loneliness is just one such indicator.[104] So too is the incidence of youth suicide.

Faced with the pain of loneliness and isolation, many people find comfort and solace in cults and a whole range of fringe, fundamentalist, and extremist movements. In a similar manner, the backgrounds and personal testimonies of young people who have joined terrorist organizations also reveal their need for friendship and support, in particular, at times of personal crisis and vulnerability. The illusion of camaraderie offered by these groups, whether cults or terrorist organizations, is powerful and seductive. It is the bait that attracts new recruits as these organizations continue to grow and proliferate across the globe.

It is a disturbing prognosis.

Who Is Vulnerable?

"Whatever any member of a cult has done, you and I could be recruited or seduced into doing under the right or wrong conditions. The majority of 'normal, average, intelligent' individuals can be led to engage in immoral, illegal, irrational, aggressive and self destructive actions that are contrary to their values or personality when manipulated situational conditions exert their power over individual dispositions."[105]

"The driving force behind the actions of terrorists tends to be the universal desire to belong to a group. That desire, when channeled by a so-called political entrepreneur, or charismatic leader, can justify almost any act; the primal need to belong allows someone to hate an enemy more than they love their own lives."[106]

The cult and terrorist phenomena cut across all racial, social, religious, and economic borders. Moreover, mental ability, social integration, success, and ambition have not prevented cults and terrorist organizations from recruiting the very members of the community who would seem least vulnerable to their influences.

According to a survivor of the Anne Hamilton-Byrne sect in Victoria, Australia, the bulk of the cult was made up of professional people. "Without their support and participation, Anne Hamilton-Byrne would not have been able to create her following. These professional people—doctors, lawyers, engineers, architects, psychiatrists, nurses and social workers—allowed her to successfully pull the wool over everyone's eyes for more than twenty years."[107]

Shoko Asahara, the architect of the sarin attacks on the Tokyo subway in 1995, was an intelligent soft-spoken father of six children. According to Professor Shinichi Nakagawa, a religion expert at Chuo University in Tokyo, "He was rational and humorous, while at the same time unsophisticated and spontaneous—traits the Japanese lost long ago."[108]

The profiles of the terrorists involved in the 9/11 attacks almost resemble a university or college list of alumni. Ayman al Zawahiri was born into an upper-class family of doctors and scholars in Egypt. He was a studious boy who joined his first Islamist group at age fourteen. He graduated from Cairo University in 1974 and received his master's in surgery in 1978.

Mohammed Atta was raised in a suburb of Cairo. Atta received a degree in architecture from Cairo University and a degree in urban planning from the Technical University of Hamburg in Germany.

Zacarias Moussaoui was born in Morlaix, France, and received his master's degree in international business affairs from London's South Bank University in 1995. By 1996, he was meeting with Islamic extremists in London and training in Al Qaeda camps in Afghanistan.

Members of other terrorist groups present similarly. Azahari Husin, the alleged master bomb-maker of the Jemaah Islamiyah terrorist organization (called the "demolition man" by Malaysian newspapers) was a British-educated engineer and former university lecturer. Husin was a property evaluation expert who turned away from his academic profession to write a new doctoral thesis on the topic of suffering. Tragically, Husin inflicted untold inhumane suffering on others.

Although everyone is vulnerable to the influences of cults or terrorist groups, there appear to be particular life conditions that make some people more vulnerable—low points at which time life becomes more difficult; illness, death of a loved one, times of crisis or soul-searching. These low points create openings for a whole range of organizations to offer assistance in the form of counseling, accommodation, or even shelter. People disenchanted with conventional religious establishments or intellectually confused over religious and philosophical issues are also vulnerable.

An unhappy relationship, conflict at home, communication problems, unemployment, and financial difficulties can also create vulnerability. Failure, loss of self-esteem, or a sense of hopelessness further weaken resistance to outside influences. Indeed, terrorists seeking to recruit suicide bombers have been known to seek out individuals who are emotionally vulnerable and have the potential to be inspired by the goals of the network.

Times of spiritual turmoil, feelings of rejection by one's chosen church, and a need to find a deeper meaning in life can also direct the searching individual to other alternatives, whose attraction is magnified as a result of these circumstances. Family situations that have never been resolved and conflicts regarding identity can help create the climate in which the helping hand of the cult or terrorist organization appears welcome.

In particular, experts on terrorism have pointed out that individuals who have a sense of uncertainty about their future may find that terrorist groups provide the sense of certainty, identity, structure, and guidance that they crave. Identification with the cause and other group members may satisfy an individual's needs for meaning and justice and afford an opportunity to bolster self-esteem.

Ami Pedahzur's research indicates that suicide bombers may be motivated by a personal commitment to a leader, group, or ideology, or a personal crisis brought about by the suffering of family, friends, or community members. "People's initial reaction to a suicide terrorist is to think the person is crazy or a religious zealot, but that's not the case," said Pedahzur. "Most suicide bombers see themselves as soldiers carrying out a mission to inflict damage on the enemy."[109]

It was the social scientist Konrad Lorenz who said that the desire to belong is so great that it matters not what one belongs to. "The instinctive need to be a member of a closely linked group fighting for common ideals may be so strong that it becomes inessential what these ideals are and whether they possess any intrinsic value."[110] Certainly, the desire to belong to a group is a powerful factor in the recruitment process. There are few other explanations as compelling as Lorenz's thesis. Indeed, in relation to terrorism, as the world struggles to understand the motives for suicide bombing and martyrdom, the desire to belong emerges as one of the most plausible explanations for this complex and disturbing behavior.

A paper written by Tore Bjorgo of the Norwegian Institute of International Affairs on recruitment issues in extremist groups sheds further light on this important issue. In particular, the paper suggests that young people who join extremist movements do so in search of friendship, community, and acceptance. Ironically, some of these organizations give the illusion of appearing to be more tolerant than mainstream society.

Bjorgo argues that the search for status and identity is also a primary reason why some young people are drawn to extremist groups. Many of these recruits are people who have failed to establish a positive identity in relation to school, sports, work, religious beliefs, or family. Thus the extremist group becomes the recruit's surrogate family, and the leader assumes the role of father to the individual.

Acceptance into the inner circle of an extremist group may prove more difficult. In their efforts to win this acceptance, some recruits appear prepared to carry out acts of violence and other crimes in order to be accepted as full members and to have their status elevated within the group.

Resistance from mainstream organizations often has the effect of further strengthening the recruit's loyalty and can lead to violence as members of the group confront detractors. Significantly, these confrontations may alter a member's perception of violence both in terms of legitimacy and familiarity with its practice.

Other researchers suggest that the people who are most vulnerable to become members of a cult are perfectionists, intolerant, and have difficulties dealing with their own aggression or acknowledging that they have hostile feelings and thoughts. Such individuals are open to being manipulated by people who promise them they will go to heaven by sending everyone who is not a member of the cult to hell.

According to Harold Bursztajn, a Harvard Medical School forensic psychiatrist who has studied mass murderers and the psychodynamics of terrorists, this type of mindset led to the Holocaust. Within a larger military conflict, Hitler and his cult of Nazis were obsessed with what they called purifying the planet of Jews and others they deemed inferior.[111] "It comes back to the concept of genocide." According to Art Rousseau, a psychiatrist who serves on the American Psychiatric Association's National Disasters Committee, "One group defines another group as so bad that they want to wipe them out. This is not something new. It goes back in time historically."[112]

One of the greatest ironies of recruitment into extremist organizations is that by belonging to a group and being submerged in its ideals, the recruit believes that he is able to express his individuality. In an insightful article into the revival of the Aum Shinri Kyo terrorist cult, Andrew Marshall, co-author of *The Cult at the End of the World: The Incredible Story of Aum*, argues that if young people are still joining Aum, it is because all the factors that created Aum's membership in the first place still exist. Japan is still a rigid society that stifles individualism and Aum exploits this. The tragedy is that the recruit's individuality is the very price he pays for membership of the group.

Clearly, recruitment to and participation in a cult or terrorist organization involves a range of complex parameters for each individual. They are critical if the means are to be found to extricate that member from the group. At the same time it is important to recognize that extrication from the group does not resolve pre-existing factors that may have contributed to making the individual vulnerable. The challenge is to address these issues at the earliest opportunity.

At the same time, evidence drawn from cases of people who have become involved in cults and terrorist organizations confirms the belief that the recruitment process does not delineate between social classes, levels of intelligence, or cultural backgrounds. Deborah Layton, a survivor of Jonestown, summed up people's vulnerability to mind control when she said, "It can happen to the best of us."[113]

Entering a Cult or Terrorist Group

"Mary Garden, whose disenchantment with Christianity led her towards the East, wrote as she landed in India, 'I glanced down at the book that I was clutching on my lap. On the cover was the strange face of Sai Baba which was mopped by black frizzy hair that his devotees likened to a halo. I felt my heart beating. I had tasted the drug of "spiritual love" and had immediately become addicted'"[114]

"Upon entry into the group, new members are indoctrinated into the Mojahedin-e Khalq terrorist organization's ideology and revisionist Iranian history. Members are also required to undertake a vow of 'eternal divorce' and participate in weekly 'ideological cleansings.' Additionally, children are reportedly separated from parents at a young age. The organization's leader Maryam Rajavi has established a 'cult of personality.' She claims to emulate the Prophet Muhammad and is viewed by members as the 'Iranian President in exile.'"[115]

One of the myths about the cult phenomenon is that people join cults, but the suggestion that people join cults is as absurd as the idea that people decide to become drug addicts.

"Cults are not merely weird groups that crazy people find attractive. Cults are massive, enduring cons. Although individuals may join cults during periods of stress and demoralization, most cult joiners are more or less within the normal range psychologically. They do not join groups because they have made a rational and informed decision that these groups will benefit them. They join because they are seduced through a gradual step-by-step process of deceit and manipulation designed to advance the leader's objectives, regardless of the harm caused to members. The centrality of sustained, exploitative manipulation distinguishes cults from benign new movements and mainstream religions."[116]

To make a truly informed decision, a person must have adequate information about the matter at hand as well as freedom to evaluate this information. The problem in relation to cults and other extremist groups is that the two criteria are not present simultaneously. At the time of entry into a cult, the individual can generally claim to have freedom of choice. He is not the subject of psychological manipulation nor is he the subject of mind control. However, he lacks detailed information about the group. Issues relating to the beliefs of the group, financial obligations for members, family contact, fundraising, or witnessing requirements are rarely discussed in the early days of cult involvement. Thus, for example, there may be no mention that the initial membership fee has little in common with required future financial commitments. There is no discussion regarding restrictive contact with the family or the harsh cult doctrine.

When one enters a cult, no mention is made of the fact that unless you are a member you are evil, satanic, or unworthy of living. No mention is made of the hierarchical nature of cults, whereby the leaders are the beneficiaries of the lower members' hard labor. Mention is not made of the estates, the properties, the sheer wealth of many of these organizations and their leaders, their business interests and their sophisticated marketing programs.

By the time a new recruit is able to fully comprehend the nature of the mission as well as the goals of the organization behind it, his ability to make a rational assessment of the organization is questionable.

The term "love bombing" has been used to describe the intensive, emotionally laden approach with which the Unification Church headed by Sun Myung Moon and also known as the Moonies recruits new members. The result is the clever and subtle creation of a new sense of belonging, security, and purpose, as well as a promise of happiness and salvation that cements the relationship between the cult member and organization. This takes place well before a recruit has the opportunity to assess the philosophy or doctrine of the cult.

Indeed, many organizations operate under numerous names that appear to have no relation to the central group. The connection between a personal development organization, est[117], and the Hunger Project or the connection between the Citizens' Commission on Human Rights and the Church of Scientology are not necessarily obvious to the uninformed observer. Similarly, only a person familiar with the workings of the Unification Church would be aware of its connection with Collegiate Association for the Research of the Divine Principle (CARP).

Terrorist organizations sometimes use sham organizations to pose as legitimate charities. There are reported cases where the entire charity is used as the vehicle to perpetrate fraud.[118] Some cults highlight their contributions in the fields of social welfare in order to sanitize their agendas.

The issue of the informed decision is particularly relevant in relation to the right of parents to intervene and extricate a loved one from a cult or extremist group. The most common criticism of any intervention is the argument that the individual is an adult who has made an informed decision to join a particular group. However, it is difficult to support the notion that the person has made an informed decision if the relevant information was not available at the time of joining.

In their slick advertising, some organizations go out of their way to attract prominent personalities, actors and performers. Many groups present images of smiling faces and happy families. These people are put on center stage as the organization attempts to broadcast its message to the vulnerable and the unsuspecting public. The Church of Scientology capitalizes on the fame of its celebrity members such as John Travolta, Tom Cruise, Anne Archer, and Priscilla Presley.[119] Scientology has also capitalized on the association of Australia's richest man, James Packer, with the organization. In 2007 Packer participated in a second wedding ceremony conducted by Scientology when he married Erica Baxter in France although it has since been reported that he is no longer associated with the Church.[120]

Terrorist organizations also welcome celebrity support with open arms. Comments of film director Oliver Stone and star Angelina Jolie in the 2004 film *Alexander* were interpreted by critics and the media as being supportive of terrorism. In an interview with famed *Hollywood Variety* columnist Army Archerd, Stone allegedly denied documented reports that the Palestine Authority used terrorism as a strategic means to get a Palestinian State. When Archerd told him of the anti-Semitic education of Palestinian youths and the glorification of suicide bombing, Stone both denied and justified it, saying, "The memories are long as are the grudges and feuds."[121]

Cults also use the concept of a living leader, guru, or master as an attraction, claiming to be more relevant and meaningful than their more abstract mainstream church rivals. A human manifestation of God is far easier to relate to than a God "out there somewhere" or something that is supposedly ever-present in every human being. A tangible leader is real and carries meaning, even if his message is one of suicide, death, and destruction. In their attempts to lure young idealistic people to their cause, cults contrast their loving communities with graphic images of political and military activity around the world highlighting the fact that religion has failed in its efforts to bring peace and stability.

In a similar way that people do not necessarily make a conscious decision to join a cult, the recruitment process to terrorist organizations can also be subtle. In an article titled "The Psychology of Terrorism," published by the Social Science Research Council, Clark McCauly, professor of psychology at Bryn Mawr College, discusses this facet of terrorist recruitment which is uncannily similar to the process of cult indoctrination. "No one wakes up one morning and decides that today is the day to become a terrorist. The trajectory by which normal people become capable of doing terrible things is usually gradual, perhaps imperceptible to the individual."

Instead of an identified initiation process, even though a very swift process of recruitment is possible, generally the recruitment of suicide bombers involves a slow process of indoctrination. It includes showing the recruit persuasive thematic material and exploiting charismatic images to help them internalize the cause of the terrorist organization. Recruits also are often shown final testimonials from "successful" suicide bombers that reinforce their commitment to die for the cause. The conditioning process may occur so slowly that the recruit is not even aware of the nature or identity of the group he has joined.

Psychologist Ariel Merari, who has studied this phenomenon extensively for many years, outlines the common steps on the path to these violent acts. First, senior members of an extremist group identify young people who, based on their declarations at a public rally, appear to have an intense patriotic fervor. Next, they are invited to discuss how seriously they love their country and hate the enemy.

The new recruits are then asked to commit themselves to being trained. Those who make the commitment then become part of a small secret cell of three to five youths. From their elders, they learn bomb making, disguise, and selecting targets. Finally, they make public the private commitment by making a videotape and declaring themselves living martyrs for Islam. The recruits are also told that their relatives will be entitled to a high place in Heaven, and they themselves will earn a place beside Allah.

Merari concludes, "The die is cast; their minds have been carefully prepared to do what is ordinarily unthinkable. In these systematic ways a host of normal, angry young men and women become transformed into true believers."[122]

In a manner very similar to cults, once recruited, the teenagers are encouraged to cut off contact with real world affairs and subjected to an intense radicalization program of memorization and repetition of the Koran. According to Vamik Volkan, emeritus professor of psychiatry at the University of Virginia School of Medicine, "their readings are carefully selected." The teachers also supply sacred sounding but meaningless phrases to be repeated over and over in chant. "These kinds of mystical sayings combined with selected verses from the Koran help to create a 'different internal world' for the 'students.'"

Although the recruitment process usually takes several weeks, Pedahzur claims that training a person can also occur very quickly, sometimes in a matter of hours. In addition to conveying basics about the operational side of a mission, the trainer must ensure the recruit's mental preparedness for the mission. The goal is to reduce the chances that he or she will change his or her mind at the last minute.

Young children are not spared the process of radicalization. Programs may involve young children being dressed up as a "shaheed" (martyr) with their parents' consents. More and more cases are coming to light of children participating in processions, wearing replicas of explosive belts and inscriptions declaring that they are martyrs. Recently the press exposed a photograph discovered in Hebron that showed a baby wearing a replica explosive belt and a headband declaring that the baby was a martyr for Allah. The indoctrination of children at such young ages serves as a prelude to their recruitment by terrorist organizations for the purpose of carrying out attacks.

Numerous factors continue to enhance the lure of cults and terrorist organizations. As their recruiting techniques and their effective advertising campaigns are stepped up and as the Internet becomes an increasingly powerful influence across the globe, the threat of enmeshment in these organizations has taken on an element of urgency. Against a backdrop of global uncertainty and ongoing fear of further terror attacks, young people will continue to find the illusory haven of these organizations as an attractive alternative to the real and often painful society that surrounds them.

Cults, Terrorism, and Religious Fundamentalism

"An event which transpired shortly after I reached Jonestown convinced me that Reverend Jones had sufficient control over the minds of the residents that it would be possible for him to affect a mass suicide.

"At least once a week, Jones would declare a 'white night', or state of emergency. During one 'white night', we were informed that our situation had become hopeless and that the only course of action open to us was a mass suicide for the glory of socialism. We were told that we would be tortured by mercenaries if we were taken alive. Everyone, including the children, was told to line up. As we passed through the line, we were given a small glass of red liquid to drink. We were told that the liquid contained poison and that we would die within 45 minutes. We all did as we were told. When the time came when we should have dropped dead, Jones explained that the poison was not real and that we had just been through a loyalty test."[123]

"We, the undersigned Muslims, wish to state clearly that those who commit acts of terror, murder and cruelty in the name of Islam are not only destroying innocent lives, but are also betraying the values of the faith they claim to represent. No injustice done to Muslims can ever justify the massacre of innocent people, and no act of terror will ever serve the cause of Islam. We repudiate and dissociate ourselves

from any Muslim group or individual who commits such brutal and un-Islamic acts. We refuse to allow our faith to be held hostage by the criminal actions of a tiny minority acting outside the teachings of both the Quran and the Prophet Muhammad, peace be upon him." [124]

The difference between a cult and a religion continues to be a contentious issue. Some experts suggest that all religions start out as cults. They contend that a religion is simply a cult which has come of age. Critics of the Catholic Church claim that the Pope's reign and authority is no different from that of a guru or enlightened master. The late Professor Margaret Singer addresses this issue in some depth.

Professor Singer states that within a monastic order even the lowliest monks have access to higher levels and can seek justice outside the order. Not so with the cults, where the hierarchal structure of the groups denies any contact between the members or followers and the higher echelons of power. Cults have a double set of ethics: within the group you must be open and honest and confess all to the leader; however, outside the group you can deceive and manipulate. In contrast, established religions and ethical groups teach members to be honest and truthful and abide by one set of ethics. [125]

Perhaps the most significant difference between a cult and a religion is the fact that in the latter the veneration is directed towards God, whereas in a cult the love and devotion is directed towards itself. The leader is either God-manifest or God himself. There is no room for question or doubt. Allied with this notion is the belief in the leader's infallibility. This belief has far-reaching implications.

Total and unquestioning commitment to a guru or a master carries the risk that in the event the leader becomes paranoid or deranged, the followers will have no choice but to remain loyal to the whims of his madness. The tragedies of Jonestown, Waco, and Heaven's Gate involved leaders who, at one time, had credibility. Jim Jones, for example, commenced his work as an ordained member of a Christian Church and was highly regarded by various U.S. dignitaries. During the 1976 American presidential campaign, Jones met with Vice Presidential candidate Walter Mondale on his campaign plane. First Lady Rosalynn Carter personally met Jones for a private dinner at the Stanford Court Hotel in San Francisco.[126]

The notion of infallibility leads many cult members to believe that life without the cult leader is unthinkable. In the event of the leader's death, the cult members may choose one of two options: to believe that the leader has not really died, as was the case with Bhagwan Shree Rajneesh, guru of the Rajneesh organization whose death was viewed as the shedding of a physical cloak, or tragically to follow their leader by committing suicide.

According to terrorism expert Anthony Stahelski, a professor at Central Washington University, in exchange for providing joiners with meaningful existences and for fulfilling their affiliative emotional needs, the terrorist leader also requests and receives unquestioning obedience from the joiners. Long-term members of the group support the leader's obedience pressure by applying conformity pressure on new joiners in order to forestall any deviation from the group's mission or values. The joiners' initial susceptibility to this intense obedience and conformity pressure makes them extremely vulnerable to the social psychological conditioning process used in violent cults.[127]

There are other differences between cults and religions. Unlike cults, religious groups support the family structure and can be credited with attempting to emphasize its importance in the face of the collapse of the nuclear family. They encourage family contact as well as the use of counseling service to heal relationships. Religious leaders do not assume the role of parents.

Religious orders will not disguise information about the true nature of the organization, its beliefs, and its structure. There are opportunities to question and to inquire. In the mainstream churches, the mission statements, the methods of appointments, and the financial records are available to the public. Cults, on the other hand, often make a deliberate effort to conceal the true nature of the group by operating under a variety of names or withholding information from the potential recruit.

The restriction on inquiry or criticism of the organization is a very disturbing feature of many cults. In his book *When God Becomes a Drug: Breaking the Chains of Religious Addiction and Abuse,* Leo Booth suggests that the discouragement of independent thinking is the primary identifying mark of a dysfunctional system. If you cannot question or examine what you are taught, if you cannot doubt or challenge authority, you are in danger of being victimized or abused.

Religions do not divide the world between the good—those who follow the religion—and the bad—those who do not follow it. This division of the world into good and evil is one of the features of cults that is almost universal. Whether the message is presented overtly or subtly, the followers are led to believe that their way is the only way; any departure from the cult and its beliefs will compromise the individual's quality of life and may be fraught with danger.

The tendency to divide the world into good and evil is also a characteristic of the "fringe churches" that are becoming increasingly popular today. These churches, which present as bona fide Christian organizations, are often guilty of the misrepresentation and deceit practiced by some of the better-known cults.

The complaint against these cults is not the fact that they are secretive, but that they are deceitful, concealing their true aims and their potential effects from followers and families.

In contrast, fraternities such as the Masons, though secretive, openly inform members that they will be taught the more secret rituals of the group as they progress. On this issue Margaret Singer said very succinctly, "A secret handshake is not equivalent to mind control."[128]

In order to show how cults differ from religions, Flavil Yeakley of Abilene Christian University administered a personality profile research device to hundreds of members of religious groups, both from established religions and cults.

Yeakley administered the tests to members of the Boston Church of Christ, the Church of Scientology, the Hare Krishnas, Maranatha, the Children of God, the Moonies, and The Way International as well as members of Baptist, Catholic, Lutheran, Methodist, and Presbyterian churches and "mainline" Church of Christ members.

The results showed that people in certain cults appeared to be all moving toward the same type of personalities regardless of the original personalities they brought with them into the group. By contrast, in the established churches, there was no indication of conformity to any type of personality. People's fundamental personality types remained intact.[129]

As clear as the line between religions and cults may be, the situation changes as one moves toward the extremes of religious fundamentalism. The 9/11 attacks together with the graphic imagery of suicide bombers in other parts of the world have again highlighted the contentious connection between religion and terrorism. According to Ian Cuthbertson, director of the World Policy Institute's Counter-Terrorism Project, it is religious extremism that serves as the most basic catalyst for the world's most radical and dangerous terrorists.

Indeed, the U.S. government long believed, even before 9/11 confirmed their worst fears, that the vast majority of terrorist attacks aimed against American interests were not going to be motivated by political or ethnic forces, but instead by the religious extremism that has inspired a new generation of more radical and absolutist terrorism. Additionally, terrorism experts have long accepted the fact that religious extremists had a greater potential to use weapons of mass destruction than their secular counterparts.[130]

Although a number of experts[131] have argued that acts of terrorism are primarily motivated by secular goals, this appears to be the minority view. Writing in *The Middle East Quarterly*[132], Jonathan Fine, a research fellow at the International Institute for Counter-Terrorism at the Hebrew University of Jerusalem argues that downplaying the religious inspiration for terrorism is both inaccurate and dangerous. Fine argues that Al Qaeda's decision to launch its attacks cannot be disengaged from ideology and the dream of renewing a lost caliphate. One of bin Laden's most important objectives was to accelerate recruitment of new volunteers for global Jihad and Islam.

As many of the cults divide the world into good and evil, so too do numerous terrorist organizations. Terrorists justify their murderous agenda by claiming that the people they are defending are facing an evil and ruthless enemy. Like cults they ascribe great power, even godlike status, to their leadership. There are stark similarities between the dedication of cult members to their masters and the total and unquestioning commitment of members of terrorist organizations to their leaders.

Most powerful of all, however, are the similarities between the methods of recruitment by both cults and terrorist organizations, in particular, the use of sophisticated mind control techniques.

Finally, it is important to draw a distinction between the mind control techniques that are used by destructive cults and terrorist groups and the conditioning processes that we are all exposed to as part of growing up. Naturally, the environment we live in, the people around us, and our own families influence and shape our thinking, attitudes, and values. Even so, this process, which creates change as we develop and mature, is not contrived to benefit an outsider or an organization. The tragic irony is that the very nature of cult practices has enabled them to reach out and attract hundreds of thousands of followers, many of whom have renounced their earlier religious affiliations.

It is a cruel reality that religions that preach tolerance and love have been supplanted by organizations that speak of hatred and division. Such is the challenge that faces the established religions today.[133]

4

Delving Deeper into Extremism

As I journeyed into various cults and sects and researched the incidence of terrorism, I was pained by stories of young and old whose lives had been shattered. These were shocking stories: the death of Deborah Layton's mother in Jonestown and the imprisonment of her brother for his alleged involvement in the murder of U.S. government officials investigating the cult;[134] the story of four teenagers who were hacked to death and eaten by a group of Satanists in Russia;[135] and the murder of 186 children in Beslan. All were tragedies that seemingly could have been avoided.

And then there was 9/11. But one month earlier on August 9, 2001, an event took place that touched the psyche of my own Australian Jewish community like no other event in living memory. On that day fifteen Israelis (seventeen if one counts the baby being carried by a pregnant woman and another victim who was left in a permanent coma) were killed and more than one hundred injured by a suicide bomber who blew himself up at a Sbarro restaurant in the heart of Jerusalem. Among the dead was fifteen-year-old Malki Roth, a former resident of Melbourne, Australia, and the daughter of highly respected community activists Arnold and Frumit Roth.

The suicide bomber, twenty-two-year-old Izz-al-Din Shuheil al-Masri from the Palestinian West Bank town of Aqabah, was the son of a successful restaurant owner from an affluent land-owning family. He was escorted to the restaurant by Ahlam Tamimi, an attractive twenty-year-old female university student and part-time journalist who had disguised herself as a Jewish tourist for the occasion. Ahlam Tamimi was sentenced to sixteen life terms.

As more than three thousand members of Melbourne's community, many of them young school children, assembled together for a memorial service, parents, families, and community leaders were forced to confront the reality of terrorism.

There were many questions and very few answers. Eight of the victims of the Sbarro terrorist attack were children, a detail that could not have gone unnoticed by the bomber as he made his way through the crowd of restaurant patrons with a guitar case slung over his shoulder packed with explosives and shrapnel.

After the suicide bombing, Palestinian university students at the An-Najah University in the West Bank city of Nablus created an exhibition celebrating the event.[136] The exhibit's main attraction was a room-sized re-enactment of the bombing at Sbarro. The installation featured broken furniture splattered with fake blood and human body parts as well as pizza slices strewn around the room. The exhibit also included an idealized portrait of the suicide bomber holding a Koran and an automatic rifle. The entrance to the exhibition was illustrated with a mural depicting the bombing.

Arnold Roth was invited to speak as Israel's representative at the Third International Congress of Terror Victims in Valencia, Spain, 2006.

"The cruelty of terrorism has become a strange kind of secret. Many politicians are too frightened to speak about it by name. And many in the communications media prefer to hide from it by the use of euphemisms and explanations which explain nothing. We, who understand better than everyone else the cruel and barbaric nature of terrorism and the high price which civilized society pays for its continuation, we the victims, must stand together. We have a solemn obligation—in the name of compassion—to remind our neighbors and our leaders that the vision of a better world demands an uncompromising struggle. A struggle to bring terror to an end. To stop the terrorists by every possible means."[137]

Terrorism and Cultism

> *"A fanatical mindset will poison people with cyanide; a fanatical mindset will fly people in (the) World Trade Center or send anthrax through the mail."* [138]
>
> *"What I find so astonishing is that most people don't realize how influenceable all humans are,"* says Margaret Singer, the former emeritus professor of psychology at the University of California at Berkeley. [139]
>
> *"Few men were more popular on the streets of Beeston than the 30-year-old family man, Sidique Kahn, one of the London bombers. Recognized by his sensible sweaters and neat, coiffured hairstyle, Khan's respectability peaked nine months ago when he visited Parliament as the guest of a local MP. There he was praised for his teaching work. Even now, those who hang about Cross Flatt's Park describe him as their mentor. He remains the man who coaxed them back into the education system; the bloke who took them on canoeing and camping trips to the nearby Yorkshire Dale; the worker in Beeston where he had nurtured their love of cricket and football."* [140]

In his highly acclaimed book *Malignant Piet Piers of Our Time: A Psychological Study of Destructive Cult Leaders from Rev. Jim Jones to Osama bin Laden,* Peter Olsson, a psychiatrist, argues that Osama bin Laden qualifies as a cult leader even though some aspects of his behavior don't fit the typical pattern. Referring to bin Laden, Olsson succinctly sums up the core destructive pattern of cult leaders as follows, "They seduce their followers with the utopian promise of empathetic resonance and healing empathy, but they end up hurting, neglecting, and killing the hungry followers, just as they themselves had felt abused, neglected, or hurt in their childhoods."

Dr. Steven Dubrow-Eichel, a Philadelphia psychiatrist who specializes in cults, points out that Al Qaeda and the Japanese Aum Shinri Kyo cult are almost indistinguishable in their adulation of a single charismatic leader. Both believe that they are fulfilling God's mission in creating a better, purer world. "Their apocalyptic vision is similar in many ways as is their sincere conviction that God sent them to purify the world," he says, "and their methods are very similar."[141]

The cult-like nature of a terrorist organization and the degree of allegiance demanded of its membership was revealed in a fascinating 1999 study undertaken by the study organization MKO Watch which examined the Mojahedin-é Khalq Organization (MKO), a listed terrorist organization by the United States state department operating in Iran during the reign of then Iraqi President Saddam Hussein. The study concluded that the MKO operated as a cult in terms of its operational tactics, recruitment, subservience to its leader, and mind control.

The study revealed that recruits had to be devoid of emotional feelings toward their loved ones and their families. They were instructed to cease contact with their families in order to become good tools to carry out terrorist acts.

Like with many cults and terrorist organizations, the recruits of MKO had to reach a point mentally at which they truly believed that they were absolutely nothing and were of no value whatsoever, the only purpose of their lives was to be sacrificed for their leader in a terrorist operation. Those who had submitted totally and could then pass this belief to others might rise higher in the system of the cult.

Within MKO, the value of an individual was measured solely by his mental, emotional, and moral proximity to the leader. As in many cults, the rank or position of the members didn't reflect their capabilities or personal talents. The main factor was the extent of dependence on and submission to the cult's leader.[142]

In a general meeting, the leader of the organization, Masoud Rajavi, proclaimed the divorce of all members from their spouses and asked them to hand over their marriage rings. The divorce of spouses and, consequently, children was a first step; the world outside with all its attractions and emotional attachments then had to be cleaned from the mind and devalued. Followers had to replace these with an alternative that was no other than Masoud and his wife Maryam Rajavi.[143]

The connection between terrorist groups and cults was highlighted immediately after the attacks of 9/11 when President Bush declared war on the cult of al Qaeda. The documentary "The Cult of the Suicide Bomber" further highlighted the connection between cults and terrorist organizations.[144]

In Australia in 2006 this connection also received attention when the then Foreign Minister Alexander Downer said the federal government was looking at the idea of deprogramming terrorists. Australian Federal Police commissioner Mick Keelty said Indonesia was using a former Jemmiah Islamiah leader to help turn extremists away from violence and extract information on terrorist operations. Deprogramming had also been used in Singapore, the United Kingdom, Pakistan, and Sri Lanka.[145]

Downer stated that in many parts of the world, Europe, the Middle East, and certainly Indonesia, governments have made an attempt to persuade extremists and terrorists held in prison to change their point of view and to understand that it is not the Islamic way to kill; it is not the Islamic way to murder. "And in some cases that process has been successful. It is something that we will give thought to."[146]

In this context he was referring to the Saudi Arabian government, which established a counseling program to re-educate and rehabilitate terrorist sympathizers as part of a self-described "war of ideas" against extremism in the kingdom. The program incorporates many traditional Saudi methods of conflict resolution and conflict management.

The centerpiece of the Saudi strategy has been dubbed the "counseling program," and is intended to assist terrorist sympathizers to "repent and abandon terrorist ideologies" by engaging them in intensive religious debates and psychological counseling. Since its inception in 2004, roughly two thousand prisoners have participated in the counseling program, and seven hundred have renounced their former beliefs and been released.[147]

Significantly, both cults and terrorist organizations gain control of recruits by demonizing the rest of the world and controlling or spinning incoming news and information. In an article titled "Terrorists Are Made, Not Born," Anthony Stahelski argues that demonization occurs when cult members become convinced that the enemy is in league with the devil and cosmic evil.

"Since most cultures define 'good' in contrast to 'evil,' demonization is a widely available conditioning strategy. Referring to the United States as the 'Great Satan' is an example of cultural demonization. Since most cultures also exonerate those who fight against and eradicate evil, demonization is simply channeled and intensified by terrorist groups. If a terrorist group member is truly convinced that old people, women, and children are evil creatures, then killing them is not just easy; it is necessary, honorable, and rewarded by those the member respects."[148]

Another feature common to both cult followers and members of terrorist organizations is their ability to live double lives. In such cases, a person may appear integrated into society while within the organization the individual dons the mantle of a follower or a devotee. Indeed, it is this feature that often frustrates the ability of families and authorities to detect an individual's involvement in an extremist group.

Mohamed Atta and the other 9/11 terrorists lived this double life. Inwardly they were committed to piety and asceticism and self-sacrifice. Outwardly they frequented bars and strip clubs, both to throw the intelligence agencies off the scent and to get a foretaste of the rewards of martyrdom. If it was bin Laden who put them up to this double life, he may well have done so with personal knowledge of the kind of guilt it would induce, and the kind of self-hatred and openness to manipulation to which the guilt could lead.[149]

The frightening reality of the double life that can be led by terrorists is also illustrated by two notorious personalities, Shehzad Tanweer and Ziad Jarrah.

Shehzad Tanweer was a popular student and also an outstanding sportsman with a shelf full of trophies. His primary passion was cricket and he rarely missed a match at the local park. Tony Miller, a fellow cricket devotee from Beeston, said, "Every time I saw him, he seemed like he was enjoying life."

His father, a former Yorkshire Police officer, owned several local businesses, including a chip shop where Shehzad often worked, joking with customers as he served them. His red Mercedes, a gift from his father, was a well-known sight around Beeston.

The news that Shehzad was suspected of being one of the terrorists involved in the London bombings of July 2005 left the people who knew and loved him reeling with shock. Their comments and statements unanimously give the impression of a quiet, sporty young man who took little interest in the news or political issues.

A shocked cousin, Safina Ahmad, wrote, "He felt completely integrated and never showed any signs of disaffection. Tanweer was never interested in foreign policy or politics." She added that she "never once saw him reading a newspaper or watching the news, nor did she see him attend any protests against Britain's involvement in Iraq or Afghanistan. Nothing could anger him. I cannot recall the last time I heard him even raise his voice."[150]

Another friend commented, "Shazzy is the best lad I have ever met. He's a top guy and a top lad. We play cricket together, he's a bowler and a batsman. He wouldn't do anything like this. He's from a very strong family. He went to university to be educated; he did a sports science degree. I saw him last week. Shehzad is a very kind person who would get along with anyone and anybody. He's the kind of guy who would condemn extremism."

It was a London daily newspaper, *The Independent*, which shed some light on the real Tanweer and his double life, one in which the terrorist was a highly focused, motivated, and independent jihadist, who spent time at a terrorist training camp in Pakistan. He was also reportedly involved with a gang in the Beeston district of Leeds that introduced radical Islam to Asian youths and engaged in battles with whites.

The training camp Tanweer visited in Pakistan was run by Harkat-ul-Mujahedeen, the "Movement for Holy Warriors," a group that had been involved in the kidnap and beheading of *Wall Street Journal* reporter Daniel Pearl in 2002 and that trained fighters operating alongside the Taliban in Afghanistan and Pakistan.

Furthermore, one of Tanweer's former associates said the bomber had received lessons in handling arms and explosives at a camp in Mansehra, a remote area near the Kashmir border. This was corroborated by sources in Pakistan, one of whom claimed that he had two stints at the camp.[151]

Several thousand kilometers away, Ziad Jarrah hailed from a well-off Lebanese middle class family with relatively liberal views. His parents sent him to a Catholic private school in Beirut called La Sagesse, where he volunteered at a camp for disabled children and helped run an anti-drug program. Later on he pursued a career in aviation at a German university and subsequently at a Miami flight school.

Ziad Jarrah was the hijacker pilot of United Airlines Flight 93. It is believed that the intention was to fly the aircraft into the White House but it crashed in a field in Pennsylvania. On the night before the hijacking, Ziad Jarrah wrote a final love note to his Turkish-German girlfriend Aysel Sengun. "I love you and I will always love you, until eternity. I don't want you to get sad. I live somewhere else where you can't see me and can't hear me but I will see you and I will know how you are. And I will wait for you until you come to me."

Debunking Myths about Terrorism

Some of the most popular beliefs about terrorism are that terrorists hail from the poorer and dysfunctional sections of society, that they have low IQs' and that they generally suffer from some form of mental illness.

The belief that poverty is a root cause of Islamist terrorism has been thoroughly discredited. Numerous studies of terrorism have debunked the notion. Islamist terrorists themselves, as well as those who live among them and know them well, have repeatedly attributed Islamist terrorism primarily to religious and ideological motivations and to the logic that against America and the West terrorism is used because it works. Abdel Aziz Rantisi, a Hamas leader, said of suicide bombing, "It is the most effective strategy for us. For us it is the same as their F-16."[152]

Marc Sageman, a senior fellow at the Foreign Policy Research Institute in Philadelphia, argues that the vast majority of terrorists come from solid middle-class backgrounds, and the leadership comes from the upper class. "This has been true for most political movements, including terrorist movements, and Al Qaeda is no different. Although Al Qaeda justifies its operations by claiming to act on behalf of its poor brothers, its links to poverty are at best vicarious."[153]

In their paper "Education, Poverty, Political Violence, and Terrorism: Is there a Causal Connection?"[154], economists Alan Kruger of Princeton University and Jitka Maleckova of Charles University in Prague conclude that any connection between poverty, education, and terrorism is, at best, indirect, complicated, and probably quite weak. They analyze opinion polls among Palestinians that show strong support for attacks against Israeli targets among students, merchants, and professionals. The unemployed were less likely to support such attacks. "If poverty were indeed the wellspring of support for terrorism or politically motivated violence, one would have expected the unemployed to be more supportive of attacks than were merchants and professionals, but the evidence points the other way," the economists conclude.

In relation to levels of levels of intelligence and levels of education, a study by Claude Berrebi, also at Princeton, shows that more than half of Palestinian suicide bombers have attended university while less than 15 percent of the general population in the same age group had any post–high school education.

Some experts argue that a higher level of education should insulate people from the effects of mind control. In contrast, Steve Hassan points out that cults intentionally recruit people who will be valuable to them, those who are intelligent, caring, and motivated.

Most cults do not want to be burdened by unintelligent people with serious emotional or physical problems. They want members who will work hard for long hours. Hassan adds that most of the former cult members he has met are exceptionally bright and educated with active imaginations, creative minds, and the capacity to focus their attention and enter deep states of concentration. "Most are idealistic and socially conscious. They want to make the most of themselves and to make a positive contribution to the world."[155]

Similarly a perusal of the profiles of terrorists involved in attacks around the world reveals a list of highly intelligent operatives. Indeed, recruiters continue to operate in universities because they prefer to recruit intelligent, skilled operatives.[156]

In their new study, "Attack Assignments in Terror Organizations and the Productivity of Suicide Bombers," two economists, Efraim Benmelech of Harvard University and Claude Berrebi of the Rand Corporation, write: "It's clear that there are some terrorist missions that require a certain level of skill to accomplish."[157]

In an article in the *New York Times* titled, "Even for Shoe Bombers, Education and Success are Linked," Benmelech and Berrebi suggest that older terrorists with better educations seem to be less likely to fail in their tasks. "Perhaps it is not surprising, then, that terrorist organizers assign them to these more difficult missions. Among Palestinian suicide bombers, the older and better-educated bombers are assigned to targets in bigger cities where they can potentially kill greater numbers of people."[158]

There has also been much debate about the mental health of terrorists. As is the case with people who join cults, current research contradicts the widely held view that there must be something wrong with terrorists, that they are crazy, suicidal, or psychopaths without moral feelings or feelings for others. Substantial research over the past thirty years has found psychopathology and personality disorder no more likely among terrorists than among non-terrorists from the same background. Interviews with current and former terrorists found few with any disorder listed in the American Psychiatric Association's Diagnostic and Statistical Manual. "Comparisons of terrorists with non-terrorists brought up in the same neighborhoods find psychopathology rates similar and low in both groups."[159]

Marc Sageman, a psychiatrist at the Solomon Asch Center, assessed the normalcy of four hundred Al Qaeda members. Three-quarters came from the upper or middle class. Ninety percent came from caring, intact families. Two-thirds had gone to college; two-thirds were married; and most had children and jobs in science and engineering. In many ways, Sageman concludes, "these are the best and brightest of their society."

David Long, former assistant director of the State Department's Office of Counter Terrorism, says that not only are terrorists not crazy, but they do not share a personality type. "No comparative work on terrorist psychology has ever succeeded in revealing a particular psychological type or uniform terrorist mindset." However, Long does assert that terrorists tend to have low self-esteem, are attracted to groups with charismatic leaders, and, not surprisingly, enjoy risk.[160]

According to Rona Fields, a psychologist who has for thirty years been examining terrorists and paramilitary members from Northern Ireland, Israel, the West Bank, Lebanon, Southeast Asia, and Africa, today's suicide terrorists share the "still-born moral and emotional development" that saw the Khmer Rouge create a bloodbath in Cambodia during the late 1970s. "Their definition of right and wrong is very black-and-white, and is directed by an authoritative director," says Fields. "There's a total limitation of the capacity to think for themselves."

Similarly, David Cante,r who has expressed reservations about the brainwashing argument, writes, "I think it is very important to realize—and we've found this in our interviews with terrorists— that they have a very cut-and-dried way of seeing the world. There are the people that they regard as part of their group and then absolutely everybody else is some external out-group that they feel legitimate to attack, and they don't understand the subtleties and complexities of society and that's why they can kill people, without any remorse, who have really not played any role at all in the problems these terrorists see themselves suffering."[161]

Clearly, the fact that the psychopathology rates of terrorists mirror the general population should not disguise the fact that many terrorists tend to have low self-esteem and are vulnerable to the influence of charismatic leaders. Similarly, there is no contradiction between psychopathology of terrorists and their tendency to view the world in black-and-white terms with a "total limitation of the capacity to think for themselves."

In a chilling reminder of our vulnerability to terrorism, Clark McCauly observes, "Indeed terrorism would be a trivial problem if only those with some kind of psychopathology could be terrorists. Rather we have to face the fact that normal people can be terrorists, that we are ourselves capable of terrorist acts under some circumstances."[162]

Tragically, cults and terrorist organization continue to fine tune their manner and techniques. The fact that "normal people" can become terrorists is a testimony to the power of mind control and thought reform as well as the havoc these phenomena can create.

The Cult of Hitler

"Karl Schnibbe joined the Hitler Youth at the age of twelve. He remembers that he 'could hardly wait for the ceremony to begin.' When Nazi leaders came recruiting eligible children in his neighborhood, he could not wait to sign up. His father did not approve, but it did not stop young Karl. 'It was very exciting. The overnight trips, campfires, and parades sounded like a great deal of fun. The boys and girls who joined the Hitler Youth had to prove not only that they were healthy,

but also that they were "true Aryans."[163]

"One of the major missions of Hitler was to get them young and take away their individuality to create group identity."[164]

Thousands of historians have explored Nazi Germany to understand how one man could mobilize an entire nation to do his bidding. In this respect there are striking similarities between the techniques that were used by the Nazi party and those used by terrorist and cult organizations.

According to Tara Woodruff of the University of California, while Nazism was never formalized as a religion, the cult of Hitler became a major aspect of the party and party life. A religious reverence for Hitler was emphasized through the use of sacred items associated with Nazism, ethical codes, special human beings, books, rituals, ceremonies, symbols, totems, and amulets. These included flags, the swastika, weapons, and even songs like the hymns in church. There were rituals or ceremonies at each stage of membership in the party that were parallel to church ceremonies and indicated different stages of involvement, like the ceremony of First Communion.

In educating budding young Nazis, propaganda proved effective. With complete control over the press, speech, education, and the then relatively new medium of the radio, the Nazis were able to influence young boys and girls in a way that had never been done before in history. Hitler, Goebbels, von Schirach, and other party leaders were able to speak directly to the youth of Germany, and many young people joined the Hitler Youth because of these speeches. During the early years the Hitler Youth held camping trips where they would sing songs devoted to the Führer, participate in athletic competitions, and enjoy the camaraderie that is found in being a part of a team. In the 1930s the Nazis often held mass rallies that celebrated not only their Führer but the new Reich as well. These rallies became almost religious in nature with all the pageantry that attends large rituals. The swastika, which had been used as a symbol of peace in other cultures, came to stand for the strength of the German state. Mystical runic symbols were used to provide the youth with a connection to the Aryan race and the Teutonic knights of old.

The Reich Youth Leaders issued patriotic appeals and used psychological ploys that would serve as an incentive for young people to join. Hitler Youth schools were set up around the country to further indoctrinate youth leaders. Education became a tool for Nazism to teach its ideas of race, religion, and duty.

The Nazis devised a new standardized school curriculum. The Nazi flag and Hitler's portrait hung in every classroom throughout Germany. In the morning, all students stood at attention dwarfed by a large Nazi flag. Classes started with "Heil Hitler!" There was no more, "Good morning, children." Any teachers who refused to teach the National Socialism agenda were dismissed. Hitler's students were also more than happy to harass and intimidate teachers who did not espouse the Nazi worldview.

All boys had to undertake a three-day cross-country hike and were also required to dive off the three-meter board headfirst into the town's swimming pool to prove their courage and devotion. After the completion of this initiation ritual, youth leaders presented their charges with the coveted Hitler Youth dagger, which bore on the blade the militaristic inscription, "Blood and Honor." All of these activities were intended to persuade the German youth that they were members of a master race that would subjugate all others.

Young German girls between ages ten and eighteen were encouraged to join the Bund Deutscher Mädel (the BDM or League of German Girls). The purpose of the BDM in the patriarchal structure of Nazism was to train girls in three important interrelated functions. The first was to serve as helpmates to the men, the second to bear them children and rear them according to Nazi values, and the third was to be faithful homemakers.[165]

Hitler needed these German girls to understand that they must procreate to continue the Aryan race and move it forward. The girls also participated in the same activities as the boys, such as hikes in the country, campfires, theatrical plays, and folk dances. The attractive uniforms were designed, much as the boys' officer-like outfits, to cultivate conformity.

Many Hitler Youth became so infatuated by their Nazi education and work ethic that they became hostile towards anyone who did not share the Nazi view of the world, including members of their own families. Since it adversely affected whether or not they could become members of the Hitler Youth, these young Germans demanded that their parents toe the party line or at least pretend to.

This replacement of family by the Nazi party was facilitated through the Hitler Youth organization and the specific youth cohort of that generation. Members of Hitler Youth were instructed to disregard familial obligations and give their loyalty to the Nazi Party. While the family traditionally provided children with the foundations of religion, this role too was usurped by the state, replacing conventional religion with the idealization of Nazism.

Ultimately, the Hitler Youth became a source of identity for young people. The Nazis were so adept at providing this identity that many under-aged applicants yearned to join the movement. The Nazis skillfully exploited the instinctual rebellion of youth against the adult world, especially teachers and parents. Young people searching for their identity and individuality believed they had found it as leaders and followers of the Hitler Youth.

Thus, the Nazis created an atmosphere where the young could come together, share the same ideals, and strive for the same goal. The seductive nature of the cult of Hitler was effective across the whole youth spectrum. Without the Hitler Youth, Nazism could never have become the murderous killing machine responsible for the greatest holocaust in the history of mankind.[166]

In 1963, the social philosopher Hannah Arendt published what was to become a classic of our times, *Eichmann in Jerusalem: A Report on the Banality of Evil*. She provides a detailed analysis of the trial of Adolf Eichmann, the Nazi figure who personally led in the murder of millions of Jews. Eichmann's defense of his actions was similar to the testimony of other Nazi leaders, that he was only following orders. What is most striking in Arendt's account of Eichmann is the description of him as an absolutely ordinary person. Half a dozen psychiatrists certified him as "normal." Arendt concluded, "The trouble with Eichmann was precisely that so many were like him, and that the many were neither perverted nor sadistic, that they were, and still are, terribly and terrifyingly normal."[167]

Philosophy of Hate—The Christian Identity Movement

"The Christian Identity movement is perhaps one of the most dangerous theological doctrines in America today. It is made all the more dangerous by the fact that so few people even realize that it exists, much less what exactly it represents. Christian Identity is the dominant theology of many active right-wing Christian groups, including many if not most Ku Klux Klan organizations."[168]

A distorted ideology, extremism, and militancy are all hallmarks of the U.S.-based Christian Identity movement that includes groups such as the Aryan Nations and its Church of Jesus Christ-Christian, Mission to Israel, Folk And Faith, Yahweh's Truth, Kingdom Identity Ministries, and White Separatist Banner.

According to the Anti-Defamation League, one of the most remarkable developments in the extreme right in the United States in the past few decades has been the rise of this obscure religious ideology known as Christian Identity. Penetrating existing racist and anti-Semitic groups and movements, it has inflamed their bigotry with religious fervor and also sparked the creation of many new groups. Adherents have committed hate crimes, bombings, and other acts of terrorism. While the movement's current influence reaches the Ku Klux Klan and neo-Nazi groups, the anti-government militia and sovereign citizen movements, most Americans are unaware of its scope or that it even exists.

Christian Identity groups or churches can be found in virtually every region of the United States. Although much weaker outside the United States, it is alleged that there are Identity groups in Canada, Ireland, Great Britain, Australia, and South Africa. Estimates of Christian Identity membership vary widely. There are an estimated two thousand to fifty thousand members in the United States and an unknown number in Canada and the rest of the British Commonwealth.[169]

The roots of the Identity movement began in England in the late 1800s under the name Anglo-Israelism. Followers believed that England and the United States were the true Israel and that white Anglo-Saxons were God's chosen people. They believed that Jews were descendants of Satan and that blacks and other non-white races, whom they called "mud people," were on the same spiritual level as animals.

The most hateful language of the movement is directed against the Jewish people who are accused of being evil, anti-Christian, un-Christian, and in control of most of the organized evil of the world, including prostitution, international slavery, international money-changing, profiteering on wars, racketeering in labor, corruption in politics, modernism in religion, atheism in the school system, promotion of lewd propaganda through theaters and picture shows, and more.[170]

The modern Identity movement in the United States surfaced in the 1950s under the leadership of Wesley Swift and William Potter Gale. When Swift, a Ku Klux Klan organizer, died in 1970, Richard G. Butler, an admirer of Adolf Hitler and the founder of the infamous Aryan Nations, proclaimed himself Swift's successor. Butler, a charismatic personality quickly became a cult figure and totalitarian leader, and was once dubbed the "elder statesman of American hate."[171] While he enjoyed a position of prevalence and power for many years, he died in 2004 following the decline and eventual bankruptcy of his organization.

Like many cults the Christian Identity has an apocalyptic vision of the world, which it ties to the Second Coming of Christ and the End Times. These End Times events are seen as part of a cleansing process that is needed before Christ's kingdom can be established on earth. Adherents believe that the Jews and their allies will attempt to destroy the white race using any means available. The result will be a violent and bloody millennial struggle, which will be a race war. The white Christian Identity believers see themselves as God's agents battling what they see as the forces of evil, Jews and non-whites.

Christian Identity followers believe they are among those chosen by God to wage this battle during Armageddon, and they will be the last line of defense for the white race and Christianity in general. To prepare for these events, it is alleged that they engage in survivalist and paramilitary training, storing foodstuffs, supplies, weapons, and ammunition. Moreover, the extent to which these organizations have been tied to murder, robber,y and kidnapping is frightening.

In August 1999, Identity follower Buford O. Furrow Jr. killed a postal worker and wounded five others after opening fire on a Jewish day-care center in Los Angeles. A month earlier, brothers Benjamin and James Williams, also Identity adherents, allegedly killed a gay couple in Happy Valley, California. And in 1985, David Tate, a member of The Order, a group that embraces Identity beliefs, killed a Missouri Highway Patrol trooper by shooting him eleven times during a routine traffic stop near Branson.[172]

As is the case with many cults and other extremist organizations, the desire to belong to the group appears central to the recruitment and indoctrination process used by these organizations. Brian Levin, a terrorism expert and a professor of criminal justice at California State University at San Bernardino, points out that adherents of the Christian Identity movement, including white supremacist groups, separate themselves from mainstream culture. "These are people who have had dysfunctional and problematic families. They get the anesthetic of a religious movement that tolerates and justifies their flaws and failures and even glorifies them. They say, 'You're not just a loner, you're a loner for a cause that's bigger than what other people understand.'" [173]

Despite the deaths of several leading figures as well as the closure of affiliated organizations, the movement has neither ceased to function nor has it decreased in its appeal to dispossessed and disenchanted young people. As is the case with cults and terrorist groups, the death or imprisonment of a leader often serves to spread a message to an audience who already feels besieged, marginalized, and alienated from society. Unfortunately, society today continues to provide a fertile feeding ground for a movement that preaches hate, prejudice, and destruction. [174]

5

The Tragic
Ramifications
of Mind Control

My transition from a student and researcher of mind control to working with families who had been affected by this phenomenon was not easy. There were very few people in Australia involved in similar work to talk to or places where I could seek advice.

Working with parents and families who had lost a loved one to a cult was disturbing. The most challenging aspect of this work was working with the victims of mind control. It was difficult to comprehend the degree of submissiveness that cult members had towards their leaders, the manner in which they spoke about them, and the lengths they were prepared to go to fulfill the leader's wishes.

Similarly, the degree to which cult members were prepared to dismiss all other religions or belief systems was astounding. To me it was one of the signs that they were indeed part of a cult. I was reminded of the words of Deborah Layton who wrote, "Alarm signals ought to go off as soon as someone tells us their way is the only right way."[175]

Most cult members I worked with freely admitted they would have murdered or committed suicide had the leader instructed them to do so. Morals and ethics were now dictated by the cult leader who had assumed control of his followers' lives.

During those years my overseas contacts proved invaluable. Gradually I also built up a network of former members of cults and other extreme groups who were willing to assist me in my work with families. Although I remained concerned about the injustices being perpetrated by the cults, I had no choice but to accept what I was seeing as a reality along with other social ills of our time and generation.

Far more difficult to accept and even more disturbing was the harm suffered by two particular segments of society, the children and the mentally ill. It was difficult to come to terms with the treatment of these often defenseless people at the hands of the cults.

I noted how children were made to feel special, not because of their innate qualities, but because they belonged to the cult. Parenting was often shared with other cult members, and family responsibilities took second place to obligations dictated by the cult.

I found myself trying to convince courts that cult-related custody battles were different from other kinds of custody battles and deserved special attention. I met with a distraught man at the Sydney airport who was waiting in vain for the return of his wife and four children who he believed had joined a Californian-based fundamentalist cult. I was also present at the emotional reunion of a father with his wife and two children after they were successfully exit-counseled from an Australian cult organization.

I watched as a former member of a U.S.-based cult was certified by the mental health authorities. I read how a former member of the Anne Hamilton-Byrne cult in Australia was committed to a psychiatric hospital as a result of the cult experience.

The plight of mentally ill followers or devotees was disturbing. Stripped of powers of rational thinking and emotionally vulnerable, these people were sucked into a system that had nothing to offer them other than a false short-term sense of security and faith. Without appropriate supports or therapy, they developed a dependence on the group, only to be thrown out and abandoned as they became unmanageable.

Terrorist groups plumbed new depths as reports emerged of their use of children and the mentally ill as suicide bombers. These horrors have now become part of the terrorist landscape.

Images of children wearing suicide vests now appear on the Internet. Videos of children mimicking the hate propaganda they have been taught at various madrassas and other fundamentalist schools are broadcast on YouTube. Young children from all walks of life around the world are confronted with this disturbing imagery; I can't help but wonder what effect this information has on them.

Somehow, the world appears to be changing. There has been a shift towards fundamentalism which is being played out in many domains. Mainstream church membership has floundered and fundamentalist groups have become more popular. Terrorist organizations have planted themselves in the heart of the human psyche as a modern day reality. Right wing extremist groups continue to assert themselves and cults re-invent themselves. I worry about the direction in which we are heading, and know there are no simple answers.

Fundamentalism and Exclusivity

"Exclusivism and elitism combined with wrong or unbalanced spiritual warfare teaching becomes a dangerous cocktail. Family members or friends who put forward another point of view are 'demonised' and seen as 'the enemy' or at best 'misled or unenlightened.' The command 'to honour your father and mother' is rationalised away."[176]

While the conduct and beliefs of a fringe or fundamentalist church need to be assessed in order to define whether the organization displays cult-like features, the nature and behavior of many of these organizations often calls for closer examination and assessment. These groups have included the Family of Love (formerly the Children of God), The Love Family (or Church of Armageddon), The Faith Assembly, the Jehovah's Witnesses, The Way International, The Boston Church of Christ, Jews for Jesus, and Marantha Christian Ministries. Other groups that draw attention include the Exclusive Brethren, The Way International, The Walk, The Grace Church, and Potter's House.

On the surface many fringe and fundamentalist churches appear to offer a more progressive form of service and devotion. Nevertheless, often, within a short period of time, a follower's dreams are shattered and his family destroyed.

The essential feature of these movements is a claim to be better than other Christians or to be true believers. The leader or leaders believe they have been called by God to be a vehicle for a special blessing to others, having received a vision or revelation from God.

A former member of a group known as The Assembly based in California commented, "Although we didn't come out and say it, in our innermost hearts we really felt that there was no place in the world like our assembly. We thought the rest of Christianity was out for lunch."[177]

One of the features of many of these fringe and fundamentalist churches is the suggestion of an attitude of superiority. For instance, the Jehovah's Witnessess For instance, the Jehovah's Witnesses proclaim that they, "invite everyone to experience the joy that comes not only from having found a religion that surpasses all others but from having found the truth."[178] The Jews for Jesus organization claims that by following its beliefs a Jew becomes complete.[179]

For a church member the conviction that the leader has been called by God creates a spirit of elitism and separatism, and further promotes the belief that only the group and its members have the right to speak on behalf of Christianity and no one else. Furthermore, because the leader has been called by God, his word is considered divine.

As a result of growing interest in the fringe church called the Order of St. Charbel mentioned earlier, the former Archbishop of Melbourne, Australia, George Pell, issued a statement in June 1997 in which he made clear that William Kamm, his teachings, and his communities have no approval of the Archdiocese of Melbourne: "Messages are alleged to have been received from this person in which great emphasis is placed on millennialism, warnings, signs, torments, days of darkness. Alleged private revelations are given importance above the revealed teachings of Scripture and the authentic guidance of the Church. Messages which are not consistent with the word of God and the constant teaching of the Church are to be rejected."[180]

For fundamentalist fringe churches the world is divided into two distinct categories, members of the group—who are the true and only believers—and the outside world—which is evil and satanic. People are either part of the group or not; there are no in-betweens. For the members, affiliation with the church represents the ultimate struggle between good and evil.

A corollary of the belief in the cult's exclusivity is found in the control it wields over its followers. In order to reinforce its control and influence a group will often impose a code of secrecy and contact with outsiders will be restricted or banned. The penalty for contact with outsiders, or breaching the rules of the group, may range from temporary suspension to total excommunication. Similarly, any questioning of the group is dealt with harshly, often with public condemnation.

The Exclusive Brethren limit socialization with outsiders, even close relatives, purposefully separating themselves from a world they see as morally corrupt. Infractions of internal rules—real or perceived—can lead to excommunication, or being "withdrawn from," and complete, permanent isolation from loved ones.

"I had a knock at the door saying that we've excommunicated you and you're not to sleep with your wife tonight," says one former senior Brethren member who fell out with the then leader more than twenty years ago and hasn't seen his wife or children since. His sons wrote to tell him they don't want to see him because he's "not right and withdrawn from and out of fellowship." He treasures these painful letters from his boys; he loves to look at their handwriting.[181]

Invariably, the exclusivity of the church and its control extends to the financial commitment of members. In Melbourne, Australia, a support group was established to assist former members of an organization called The Grace Church. Spokesperson for the group, Genna Piraino, claimed that he had lost $200,000 after he unwittingly donated money to the church's leader, Reverend Niel Thomas. "I even sold my country property, giving him the entire proceeds so they could build a college. It was never built."[182]

Reverend James Ridgeway, Principal of Kingsley College, said that Reverend Thomas had left a trail of "broken people, used and disillusioned, if not discarded." He claimed that the Reverend Thomas's activities should be condemned by fellow Christians because of the patent and continual unethical practices which characterize aspects of his leadership.[183]

Many groups have a language of their own with strong emphasis on subjective experience. Often particular phrases will become part of their speech: "words from the Lord," "God showed me," "the Lord told me," and "I sense the Spirit"[184] The spiritual elitism of such churches can also be seen in the terminology they use to refer to themselves, often using inflated names such as "God's Green Berets," or "God's End Time Army," or "the Faithful Remnant."

Control is further exercised in some cults by creating a crisis mentality suggesting that the End Times are near, that soon there will be a showdown between good and evil and that only the group will survive the showdown. In May 1998, William Kamm warned his followers that many wars would break out soon, and that this would be in preparation for the Great War that lies waiting to engulf the whole earth. "Be not afraid to sacrifice your lives; be not afraid to give of yourself to God," he said. A former member described, "We all believed him. I went out and bought a crossbow and I was one of the last people to arm themselves."[185]

In many of these groups, the attitude to women is oppressive. Women are often excluded from the actual service and the process of decision-making. With their roles often defined as serving the male population, women carry second-rate status and are often exploited by the male leadership. In 2005, William "Little Pebble" Kamm, leader of the Order of St. Charbel, based near Nowra in rural Australia, was sent to trial on four charges of aggravated indecent assault and one of aggravated sexual intercourse with a fifteen-year-old girl.

The court has heard that the alleged victim had become "mystically married" to Kamm and was one of twelve queens and seventy-two princesses "designated" by the Virgin Mary to conceive a new race with him.[186]

As Ronald Enroth writes in his work *Churches that Abuse*, "Unlike physical abuse that often results in bruised bodies, spiritual and pastoral abuse leaves scars on the psyche and soul."[187]

Ex-members of fringe churches, like other former cult members, often struggle to explain how difficult it is to escape the influence and control of the group. Mr. and Mrs. Ken Wallis left the Exclusive Brethren in February 1998 after becoming disenchanted with the church. They took with them their four youngest children, but their four oldest daughters decided to stay with the church and have since cut off all contact with their parents. "If you have not been part of the Brethren, you cannot understand what it is like," Mrs. Wallis said. Mr. Wallis said that he would not give up the quest to have his daughters back. "We love them very, very much. They have been told that we are evil but we have never done anything wrong and never will."[188]

The belief that their particular leader has been chosen by God is common to terrorist groups as well as fringe churches and becomes a powerful rallying point for the organization. According to *The 9/11 Commission Report*, Osama bin Laden saw himself as called "to follow in the footsteps of the Messenger and to communicate his message to all nations, and to serve as the rallying point and organizer for a new kind of war to destroy America and bring the world to Islam."[189] Bin Laden's spin doctors have gone a long way to demonstrate the omnipotence of the terrorist leader and show that he closely resembles the personage of the Prophet Mohammed.

One videotape of bin Laden has been the focus of much attention in intelligence circles. In it bin Laden stands before a dry-erase board that has written on it the name "Mahdi" meaning "awaited enlightened one." Bin Laden has encouraged this belief about himself among his followers. Indeed, the escape of bin Laden from Afghanistan in 2001 and his success in eluding capture or death ever since has elevated him as a symbolic firebrand for radical Islam.

By presenting himself as the divinely protected millennial destroyer of the Great Satan America, bin Laden has molded his public image to resemble the holy warlord figure of the Mahdi. He completed the casting of this apocalyptic drama by provoking America to present itself as a belligerent empire. These machinations reveal a truth of devastating consequence for Al Qaeda's media campaign, the righteous appearance of bin Laden's revolutionary movement serves to disguise the true motive for his planned nuclear holocaust, Messiah pretension, the abominably sinister act of vanity behind the 9/11 war.[190]

The exalted status that Osama bin Laden has achieved among the Islamic diaspora of Europe is significant. Xavier Raufer, professor at the Paris Institute of Criminology, University of Paris, refers to the mythology that has been built up around bin Laden as a sort of Islamic Robin Hood. "At a time of significant agitation and frustration in the Islamic community, bin Laden gives them a sense of empowerment. By urging Muslims everywhere to strike a blow against the West, he offers them a catharsis. This emergence of bin Laden as an iconic Islamic hero is very troubling."[191]

Michael S. Swetman, president of the Potomac Institute for Policy Studies in Arlington and author of *Osama Bin Laden's Al Qaeda: A Profile of a Terrorist Network*, suggests that to his followers bin Laden is a charismatic though quiet and reserved man. "He is almost worshipped ... very much like an ayatollah. He recruits young people, indoctrinates them and brainwashes them to the point where they are willing to give their life to attack the United States and Israel."[192]

In a chilling statement, Siraadj Munir, writing on islamfortoday.com, says about life after bin Laden. "As an occulted leader, Osama will become a new Mahdi, inspiring his minions to continue the Jihad, to continue to bring terror to innocent victims and will at the same time blacken the name and reputation of Islam."[193]

Personality Breakdown

"Many contemporary management training schemes have been in-fluenced by the human potential movement which works to 'strip away the societal impact of a personality and get to the core of human good-ness.' Unfortunately, for some programs this means trying to expose and re-work people's emotions. In group settings this often requires the violation of personal confidentiality. They (the programs) can cause more problems than they solve."[194]

For the families of members of cults or terrorist organizations, the involvement of a loved one in anti-social and potentially dangerous activities is a nightmare. As they begin to grasp the concept of mind control, they realize that their loved ones are no longer the persons they once were. In many senses they have suffered some sort of personality breakdown.

This issue of personality breakdown has attracted attention, in particular, as a result of the growth of numerous psychotherapeutic and personal development groups around the world. While many offer substantial benefits to the participants, others provide particular reasons for concern.

As a prime example, the organization Money & You has drawn attention because of its controversial methods. The group claims to offer courses in business management and training. Critics of the organization claim that the very carefully orchestrated program has the effect of deconstructing the participant's personality and then having it reconstructed through the values and the beliefs of the organization. Allegations claim that participants in the courses become entangled in an organization that manipulates the mind.

Money & You has attracted clients from both business groups and government authorities. An Australian Broadcasting Commission Four Corners program in 1993 documented the participation of the New South Wales Fire Brigade in Money & You programs.[195] The Brigade said that twenty-eight senior officers and numerous other lower-ranking officers had completed the course. Although it admitted that not everybody was satisfied, the course had provided benefits to others.

Some of the officers who had participated were particularly critical. "It's not for them to attempt to strip away a person's religion or conviction purely with the idea of replacing it with their own. My observation is that to become part of the dynamics and euphoria which were going on, you had to succumb to their ideas and values. I think the undercurrent of the course is to create a cult following."

Reverend David Millikan, an Australian Uniting Church theologian who investigated the organization, expressed particular concern about the emotional implications of the group processes. One activity known as the "blocks game" involved small groups of people sitting around tables. They were given a set of colored wooden blocks with the objective of organizing them in such a way that they represented the emotions of the group. Although the activity may have started out as a benign group experience in the early hours of the evening, this was certainly not the case when at 3 A.M. the groups were still trying to complete the task. With anxiety and tension rising, it was clear that "this was a technique to drive people further and further into themselves."

Millikan claimed that by this time people were becoming so emotional they were losing control of their minds. The level of frustration had them at the breaking point. The room was filled with the sounds of sobbing and screams. Virtually everybody was crying. According to one participant, "Some were on the edge of a nervous breakdown, and that's when it really started to worry me. I thought, there's more to this than personal development and management style. There was something else which really scared me at the time."

The television documentary referred to above featured graphic scenes of some groups hugging and embracing each other after having found the answer to the blocks game, while others agonized and suffered for not having reached a solution. Four Corners staff were asked to leave the hall at 3:00 A.M. Millikan claimed that what began as a course in business and planning had moved into the world of belief and religion.

Another former member interviewed on the program summed up his views thus: "I haven't been subjected to brainwashing but I think if I were, this would be pretty close to what it would be like. Your resistance is lowered to a point where you start losing sight of your own values and your own convictions and of course you're being constantly pounded with these ideas from the people that are presenting the show. The experience was unique. It frightened me. For several weeks I felt I was under assault. I am concerned about some of the people who walk away from the course."

Other participants in Money & You were more direct in likening it to a cult, claiming that the only effective way of parting company with the group was by exit counseling. One lawyer who had been with Money & You told how he had been prepared to leave his wife and family. The couple had newborn twins and a thirteen-month-old baby. He claimed the group had become part of his business and virtually assumed control of every aspect of his life. He was eventually exit-counseled and left the group. "I wasn't told that NLP (neuro-linguistic programming) would be involved. I wasn't told 'we are going to put you in a trance and you'll become highly suggestible,'" he said. Another participant was more direct, claiming the group was responsible for the breakdown of her personality; "Years later, I am just beginning to recover."

The issue of personality breakdown is as relevant to terrorist organizations as it is to religious cults. Experts suggest that some level of personality breakdown is necessary in order to counteract a person's strongest instinct, the urge to survive. In his book *Why People Die by Suicide,* Thomas E. Joiner, professor of psychology at Florida

State University, argues that those who kill themselves must first become fearless. "They somehow shed their natural horror of death and the equally natural fear of the pain that's often involved."

In a manner similar to the operation of personal development cults, the deconstruction of a recruit's personality lies at the heart of the carefully scripted programs prepared by a terrorist organization. Through persistence such an organization extinguishes the potential suicide bomber's natural feelings and turns him or her into something less than human, a non-person, a smart bomb, or a missile rather than an individual.

As terrorist recruits gravitate away from their earlier affiliations and associations, recruits are led to give up any values, beliefs, attitudes, or behavior patterns that deviate from the group values and expectations. Recruits are expected to ignore their own personal sense of right and wrong if it is different from that of the leader. Furthermore, the member's broader view of reality—a concept of how the past, present, and future fit together to create the social world—becomes aligned with that of the leader. Eventually, the recruit is no longer concerned about his own unique qualities but instead becomes an anonymous part of the bigger picture.[196]

Much of this is achieved through obedience training that enforces unquestioned submission to the will of authority. The individual develops a behavioral intention to act on command by repeatedly agreeing "to cheat, to forge, to blackmail, to corrupt the minds of children, to distribute habit-forming drugs." It was the author C.P. Snow who wrote that more crimes against human nature were committed in the name of obedience than in the name of rebellion.[197]

The deconstruction of the recruit's personality and the adoption of a new cult persona enables him to identify emotionally with his small cell, viewing it as a family for whom he is willing to die as a mother for her child or a soldier for his buddies. Like good advertisers, the charismatic leaders of martyr-sponsoring organizations turn ordinary desires for family and religion into cravings for what they're pitching.

Within the new personality fear is replaced by a sense of pride and joy. In the Gaza City neighborhood of Zeitoun, a strike by the Israeli air force killed two Hamas members, including the son of senior Hamas lawmaker, Khalil al-Haya. Visiting the morgue at Gaza City's Shifa hospital, Khalil al-Haya said he was proud that his son, like many of his relatives, had lost his life for the Hamas cause. "I thank God for this gift," he said. "This is the tenth member of my family to receive the honor of martyrdom."[198]

Following intensive training and indoctrination, Marwan Abu Ubeida asked his commander to consider him for a suicide mission. "When he finally agreed," Marwan recalls, "it was the happiest day of my life." There are, he says, scores of names on that list, and it can be months before a volunteer is assigned an operation. But at the current high rate of attacks, Marwan hopes he will be called up soon. "I can't wait," he says, rubbing his thumbs with his fingers in nervous energy. "I am ready to die now."[199]

The Destruction of Innocence— Mind Control and Children

"Following 'extremely malicious and unprecedented sex offenses,' Pastor Tamotsu Kin, 62, former head of the Central Church of Holy God in Japan, attempted to cover up his crime by forbidding the girls to talk about his offenses and by making them sign a vow saying that he had committed no offense against them.

"The trial against Kin which resulted in him receiving a twenty year prison sentence focused on whether he had controlled the girls through preaching and other means of influence, making them unable to resist his advances. In the ruling, the judge pointed out that Kin was a symbol of awe and respect close to God for the girls as he convinced them that if they did not obey his instructions, they would go to hell and suffer forever. The judge acknowledged the girls had had no alternative but to obey because they could not refuse his requests."[200]

"In the Palestinian territories, there currently exists a 'cult of martyrdom.' From a very young age children are socialized into a group consciousness that honors 'martyrs,' including human bombers who have given their lives for the fight against what is perceived by Palestinians to be the unjust occupation of their lands. Young children are told stories of 'martyrs.' Many young people wear necklaces venerating particular 'martyrs,' posters decorate the walls of towns and rock and music videos extol the virtues of bombers."[201]

The death of almost three hundred children in the Jonestown tragedy in 1978 shocked the world. In his book *Children of Jonestown*, child advocate and journalist Kenneth Wooden investigated child abuse in Jim Jones's Peoples Temple. Wooden wrote: "Physical abuse of the young was part of the routine at Peoples Temple. As Jones began to exercise control, children were beaten if they failed to call him Father or were otherwise disrespectful or if they talked with peers who were not members of Peoples Temple. Belts were used at first, then were replaced by elm switches. Mild discipline gave way to making young girls strip almost nude in front of the full membership and then forcing them to take cold showers or jump into the cold swimming pool at the Redwood Valley Church."

In 1983, Australian community services authorities were notified about the existence of a group of children who had been completely isolated from their families in a cult known as The Family led by a woman called Anne Hamilton-Byrne. Their hair had been dyed blond and they had been given new names, all carrying the leader's surname as their own.

In her book *Unseen, Unheard and Unknown*, Sarah Hamilton-Byrne, a former member of the group, wrote, "We believed the Aunties could kill us because we had been so bad. We didn't know that it was illegal to punish us as they did, let alone kill us. We didn't know there was a society out there that could stop them; that there were any rules apart from theirs. To us they had complete control over life and death."

In 1990, six Philadelphia children whose parents were associated with The Faith Tabernacle died of complications from measles. According to a local health official, with one exception, the children could have been saved with medical care.[202]

In 1992, the Department of Community Service was involved in a series of simultaneous raids on Children of God sects in the Australian states of Victoria and New South Wales. A witness involved in the raids said that the government was concerned about significant harm to the children. "There was a worry that their emotional development may be at risk. They were subject to extreme isolation, which caused them to be deprived of ordinary children's experience," the witness said. The children had no outside contacts, no recreation facilities, and were forbidden contact with members of their extended families, especially those who may have expressed concern about the sect. The witness said that the children had told her they must smile all the time. "Crying is not a response these children are allowed," she said.

In a tragic irony, following the Beslan massacre in Russia in September 2004 that took 331 lives, including 186 children, at least eleven mothers of the dead turned to a cult that promised to resurrect their children for money. According to the news service Izvestia, the self-proclaimed cult leader Grigory Grabovoi, who boasted a following of four hundred disciples, predicted that the Beslan children would be resurrected in October 2005.[203]

Controversy regarding the Steiner educational system surfaced in Australia in July 2007 when a number of parents contacted the media with concerns over whether the Steiner education system was based on a holistic or spiritual model. One parent, Ray Pereira, reported that he could not believe what he was hearing from the school faculty. His son's teacher had informed him that his child had to repeat prep because the boy's soul had not fully incarnated. "She said his soul was hovering above the earth," Pereira said. "And she then produced a couple of my son's drawings as evidence that his depiction of the world was from a perspective looking down on the earth from above. I just looked at my wife, and we both thought, 'we are out of here.'"[204]

The leader of a Canadian cult called The Science of the Soul urged his followers to blindfold their newborn children until the age of five in order to prolong the children's innate purity. A former devotee said that while in the group's ashram in India she witnessed children being forced to meditate ten hours a day in total isolation.[205]

While cults and mind control continue to take their toll among the young and impressionable, the recruitment of young people into terrorist cults to become suicide bombers has raised community concerns to new levels. The images of young people wearing suicide belts and speaking on video prior to embarking on their murderous missions are chilling reminders of the degree to which the human mind can be bent and manipulated.

Indeed, some terrorist organizations believe you can't start recruiting too early. A web page for children run from Lebanon carries a feature called "Shahid (martyr) of the Week." A recent installment, "A Palestinian Girl's Heroism," concerns a fictional child who leads Israeli soldiers to their death in a minefield, dying with them. The illustration shows her smiling, happy in her after-life.[206]

Tragically, most suicide bombers are recruited in their teens with the same methods used by many of the better known religious cults and sects. According to Vamik Volkan, emeritus professor of psychiary at the University of Virginia School of Medicine, "Most suicide bombers in the Middle East are chosen as teenagers, 'educated,' and then sent off to perform their duty when they are in their late teens or early to mid-twenties."[207]

According to the Washington-based Center for Defense Information, in 1998, the Kurdish Workers Party (PKK) was believed to have three thousand child soldiers in its forces, more than 10 percent of which were girls. Reports indicate that the PKK has used children since 1994 and even developed a children's battalion named Tabura Zaroken Sehit Agit. A child as young as seven was reported in the PKK's ranks. The Patriotic Union of Kurdistan

(PUK), another Iraqi opposition group, is also believed to use children as soldiers. Reports have indicated children as young as ten serving within the PUK's ranks.[208]

In June 2002, a sixteen-year-old Palestinian boy by the name Issa Bdir was dispatched by the al-Aqsa Martyrs Brigades to carry out a terror attack in Rishon Letzion, a suburb of Tel Aviv. After dying his hair blond so as to appear European, he entered a crowded pedestrian mall packed with elderly people and foreign workers and blew himself up, killing two Israelis including one teenager and wounding more than thirty others. At that point Bdir became the youngest person ever to successfully complete a suicide mission in Israel.[209]

In August 2003, two Kashmiri Muslim boys, aged thirteen and seventeen, were kidnapped at gunpoint by the Lashkar-e-Toiba terrorist organization. The boys were among hundreds of Muslim youth who had been forcibly recruited and trained to commit acts of terror against the Indian military and civilian populations. The kidnappers were most likely responding to the dictates of the terrorists who ordered local villages "to contribute one recruit each to the organization, or face reprisals."[210]

On November 1, 2004, Amar al-Faar, another sixteen-year-old Palestinian boy, entered Israel through a gap in the security fence. He carried out a suicide bombing in the densely populated Carmel outdoor market in Tel Aviv. The boy's attack killed four Israelis and wounded thirty-two, six of them seriously. Al-Faar was recruited by members of the Popular Front for the Liberation of Palestine (PFLP), a neo-Marxist faction of Yasser Arafat's Palestine Liberation Organization (PLO). In interviews following the attack, al-Faar's mother condemned the terrorists who recruited her son, claiming, "It's immoral to send someone so young. They should have sent an adult who understands the meaning of his deeds."[211]

In June 2007, The International Security Assistance Force (ISAF) in southern Afghanistan revealed that soldiers defused an explosive vest that had been placed on a six-year-old who had been told to attack Afghan army forces in the east of the country. The boy was spotted after appearing confused at a checkpoint. The vest was defused and no one was hurt. [212]

In a highly publicized story, fourteen-year-old Shakirullah Yassin Ali was arrested in Afghanistan and convicted for planning to carry out a suicide bombing. He says Muslim radicals lied and tricked him. "I have been detained for trying to commit a suicide attack," he says. He said that his recruiters told him it was his mission as a Muslim to kill British and American soldiers because they were killing Muslims. Shakirullah now sits in a crowded classroom at a detention facility in Kabul; he will serve at least five years in detentions and will be transferred into an adult prison in a couple of years. His only wish is to see his parents again. "I miss my parents, my mom and dad," he says. In relation to his recruiters, Shakirullah simply says, "They cheated me."[213]

The degree to which terrorist ideology can determine the fate of a family is perhaps best illustrated by the action of a Palestinian woman, Umm Nidal, who sent three of her six children to become suicide bombers. All perished during their missions. In defending her actions during a television interview she said, "I love my children, but as Muslims we pressure ourselves and sacrifice our emotions for the interest of the homeland. The greater interest takes precedence to the personal interest." Significantly, she was later elected to the Palestinian legislature on the Hamas ticket.[214]

Within this very dark and dangerous world, the process of radicalizing children starts well before actual indoctrination. The preparatory steps towards indoctrination are a crucial part of the process. One of the most colorful and disturbing examples of this radicalization was the creation in April 2007 by Hamas of a Mickey Mouse look-alike character named Farfur (butterfly). The character called for Muslim world domination and encouraged children to commit martyrdom. Farfur and a female co-host instructed young viewers on Hamas's militant brand of Muslim piety and urged children to support armed resistance against Israel.

The involvement of young people in acts of terrorism and the means by which they are recruited and indoctrinated highlight the need for counter education programs as well as appropriate legislation to reverse this process. Nevertheless, any such action calls for a comprehensive understanding of the workings of mind control and its impact on young people.

The magnitude of this task is highlighted by a number of surveys. According to Shafiq Maslha, a clinical psychologist who teaches in the education program at Tel Aviv University, 15 percent of Palestinian children dream of becoming suicide bombers. According to Eyad Sarraj, a Palestinian psychiatrist and director of the Gaza Community Mental Health Program, a survey his group made found that 36 per cent of Palestinians over twelve aspired to die a martyr's death fighting Israel. Other surveys have been even more disturbing.[215]

Tragically, the recruitment of children continues. In November 2007, the head of Britain's intelligence services warned that children as young as fifteen were becoming involved in terrorist-related activity. Jonathan Evans, the chief of MI5, told a gathering of newspaper editors in Manchester, "As I speak, terrorists are methodically and intentionally targeting young people and children in this country. They are radicalizing, indoctrinating, and grooming young, vulnerable people to carry out acts of terrorism."[216]

The effects of this process can be devastating. In 2007 the Pakistani army surrounded the pro-Taliban Red Mosque, a religious school complex in the heart of Pakistan's capital where hundreds of children were being held as virtual hostages in a stand-off between militants and the government. Writing in Times Online, Dean Nelson pointed to evidence that many of the children had been brainwashed into a cult of martyrdom, and that the authorities feared that some were being prepared to be suicide bombers. In barely eight weeks, ten-year-old Saima Kahn, one of the children held in the complex, had been transformed from a religious but fun-loving girl to a jihadi, grimly craving martyrdom.

In 2006, Amnesty International put out a statement condemning the use of children in terrorist activities. In part it read, "Amnesty International has repeatedly condemned suicide bombings and other attacks against civilians by Palestinian armed groups as crimes against humanity. Using children to carry out or assist in armed attacks of any kind is an abomination. We call on the Palestinian leadership to publicly denounce these practices." It went on to say, "Palestinian armed groups, including Hamas, Islamic Jihad and al-Aqsa Martyrs Brigades must put an immediate end to the use or involvement of any kind of children in armed activity."

It is important to remember the degree to which these young indoctrinated children are victims of exploitation and opportunism. The terrorist recruiters exploit their youthfulness, naiveté, blind idealism, spontaneity, and misplaced admiration for a charismatic leader. Their inability to consider the consequences of their actions is regarded as an asset by their recruiters. Cheryl Benard, a senior political analyst with the Rand Corporation and associate professor at the University of Vienna, says, "whether they succeed or fail, are themselves killed, go on to kill again or land in detention, their acts are likely to have deep consequences for their subsequent mental and physical well being."[217]

There may be divisions in relation to the issue of adults becoming involved in cults or extremist groups and whether their decision to join was an informed decision. There can be no such argument regarding children who have been exploited during their most vulnerable years.

Victimizing the Mentally Ill

"Early last year David was hospitalized. He was diagnosed with schizophrenia. Our family spent many months grieving and coming to terms with David's illness. We were surprised when, nine months later, he had improved and was well enough to leave hospital. Several

weeks ago, we received a letter from him telling us he had joined an Eastern group and would be leaving for India in a few days. He wrote that he had been told to cease taking his medication. We have tried to contact him without success. A boarder who was living with him believes he is already in India."[218]

"A terrorism suspect who police say wanted to die in an attack was described as schizophrenic in a psychiatric report prepared less than two months ago. Khaled Sharrouf, 24, was diagnosed as a schizophrenic four years ago and suffers from a mental illness that would probably have influenced his behavior in making the alleged remarks, according to the author of one of the reports. Revelations of Sharrouf's mental state came to light a day after police released a statement describing how he and seven others they allege were planning terrorist attacks in Australia, had purchased chemicals that could be used to make bombs and had travelled to properties near Bourke in New South Wales to prepare for their assaults."[219]

Although studies show that the majority of people being drawn into cults or terrorist organizations do not suffer from a mental illness, there are exceptions. The possibility of mentally disturbed people being attracted to a cult or terrorist organization represents an added nightmare for families and friends. Like the child who has become ensnared in a cult, the mentally ill person is often powerless to resist the overwhelming pressure of the group.

For these people, the issue is significant as these groups have the potential to become a haven for the mentally ill and the emotionally unstable. Health professionals as well as families who have had to deal with mentally disturbed individuals are aware of the fact that mental illness can be accompanied by delusions of a religious or spiritual nature. It is not unusual for people suffering from schizophrenia to associate the hearing of voices with a holy calling or a special relationship with God. People suffering from these conditions may be particularly vulnerable to cults.

Throughout the world there has been a trend towards not institutionalizing of mental health sufferers and an attempt on the part of authorities to reintegrate these people into the community. Invariably, these changes have created a far greater level of exposure to the deceptive practices of individuals and groups who choose to take advantage of people suffering from a mental illness.

In the attempts of these people to make sense of their lives, the attractiveness of a cult can be magnified. Where independent living can be a day-to-day struggle, the offer for accommodation, food, and comfort can be most inviting. If, in addition, a cult is able to offer counseling and support, the picture is complete.

These concerns were highlighted after considerable media exposure regarding an Australian organization called Mercy Ministries in March 2008. On its website, Mercy Ministries claimed to treat women from the age of sixteen to twenty-eight by "providing homes and care for young women suffering the effects of eating disorders, self-harm, abuse, depression, unplanned pregnancies and other life controlling issues." But three former patients told an Australian newspaper that the programs involved "emotionally cruel and medically unproven techniques," such as exorcisms and "separation contracts" between friends. Girls reportedly left the Mercy center suicidal after being told they were possessed by demons.[220]

Former residents said no medical or psychological services were provided, just an occasional, monitored trip to a doctor, where the consultation took place in the presence of a Mercy Ministries' staff member or volunteer. Patients of Mercy Ministries claimed that the program focused on prayer, Christian counseling, and expelling demons from in and around the young women, who say they begged the organization to let them get medical help for the conditions they were suffering, which included bipolar disorder, anxiety disorders, and anorexia. These requests were denied.[221]

In relation to the accompaniment by Mercy Ministries staff on doctors' visits, the president and chair of the Australian Medical Association's ethics committee, Rosanna Capolingua, said patients must be able to talk freely to their doctor about how they are feeling, without the potential influence of a third party.

"And even if the doctor did ask the patient whether they had consented (to the presence of a third party), the patient may not be able to answer. They are already vulnerable, they are coming in potentially under duress and they have another layer of fear on board … they might not have the courage to answer."[222]

In response to the complaints of former residents, Mercy Ministries executive manager of programs Judy Watson said that staff address the issues that the residents face from a holistic client-focused approach: physical, mental, emotional. The program is voluntary and all aspects are explained comprehensively to the residents and no force is used."[223]

While there are those who argue that the environment provided by such organizations may be preferable to the absence of any care at all, the reality is that for some members who don't conform with the strict rules of these programs, such comforts are often short-lived.

After eight months as a patient at a "medical" facility run by a fundamentalist church, one woman was thrown out because "she didn't want to get better." With no place to go and her hopes for recovery completely dashed, she begged for compassion but received none. She spent the last night sleeping on the floor and was forbidden to talk to any other patients. She wasn't even allowed to say goodbye.

In relation to cults, the anguish of families whose loved ones have joined these groups is exacerbated by their awareness of the mental health issues of the person. Many cults take an anti-medication stance and the denial of medication to the member can serve to increase the family's anxiety. The problem is further magnified by the person's isolation from family, medical practitioners, and mental health professionals.

Although the insular nature of cults and the insistence that any psychological or emotional problems be dealt with "in house" are potentially dangerous for any cult member, the situation of the mentally ill is even more serious. Some cults brand all form of psychological or psychiatric intervention as evil.

Noticeable in its vehement opposition to the psychiatric profession is the Church of Scientology. The Citizens Commission on Human Rights (CCHR) which was founded by the Church of Scientology in 1969 includes a series of brochures on its website which condemn the practice of psychiatry. They include: *Chaos and Terror Manufactured by Psychiatry; Massive Fraud: Psychiatry's Corrupt Industry; Harming Artists: Psychiatry Ruins Creativity; Child Drugging: Psychiatry Destroying Lives.* [224] Similarly, in 1996 *The Cult Observer* reported the appearance of four Scientology-based magazines in a glitzy, bizarrely illustrated series: *Psychiatry, Education's Ruin; Psychiatry: Victimizing the Elderly; Psychiatry's Betrayal* (about creating racism); and *Psychiatry's Rape* (on psychiatry and female patients).[225]

In its efforts to support a bill in the Florida legislature that would strip power from child abuse investigators, a spokesperson for the Citizens Commission on Human Rights said, "No activity in modern American history is as reminiscent of the destructive and terrifying abuse of power of the psychiatrists in Nazi Germany as that of the psychiatrists and other mental health practitioners currently operating in the child protective system."[226]

Whereas there may be avenues whereby parents are able to approach relevant statutory bodies to assess child exploitation or negligence, these avenues do not exist, as a rule, with adults. In serious situations there is the risk of suicide or other self-destructive behavior over which the family has no control. There is also the possibility of individuals doing harm to others as a result of their illness.

The cult's mind-altering techniques, the reframing of values, and redefinition of the world are themselves reason for grave concern. However, when these changes are superimposed onto a troubled mind or fragmented personality, the results can be tragic.

The exploitation of mentally ill people by terrorist groups is a more recent and frightening development. In a report of a suicide bombing in Iraq in February 2008, it was alleged that the act was carried out by two adults with Down's syndrome. It appeared that they were unable to comprehend the nature of the mission that took their lives along with seventy-three other victims.

In May 2008, the British intelligence service MI5 expressed concerns that Islamic terrorists were recruiting mentally ill people to carry out suicide attacks. According to MI5, people with mental disabilities were not only easier to manipulate but also less likely to arouse suspicion, and if they were white Muslim converts, they would be even less likely to be noticed in Britain.

"It is a grotesque concept but they are using people who are clearly mentally subnormal. We know they have clever radicalizers who will take advantage of anyone they think they can manipulate, whether they have an IQ of 60 or 140," an MI5 counterterrorism official told *The Sunday Times* in London.[227]

According to the official, the case of Nicky Reilly, who was held over a nail bomb attack last week in Exeter, was one such example. A twenty-two-year-old Muslim convert, Reilly is said to have been suffering from Asperger's syndrome—a form of autism—and had spent time detained in a mental health hospital. He had been described as a shambling introvert with the mental age of a ten-year-old, a product of a troubled working-class home who developed mental problems in adolescence.

"Our investigation so far indicates Reilly, who had a history of mental illness, had adopted the Islamic faith," said Tony Melville, a deputy chief constable of the Devon and Cornwall police force. "We believe, despite his weak and vulnerable illness, he was preyed upon, radicalized and taken advantage of."

"Here was a man with a borderline IQ and mental problems who was apparently recruited by extremists," said a senior British anti-terror official. "It's a method that we are aware of in Iraq. This shows we have to expand our attention to new areas where radicalization can take place. Not just prisons or schools, but mental institutions and the mentally ill."[228]

Other security officials claim that Al Qaeda is exporting the tactic of targeting mentally challenged people. The tactic was developed in Iraq where disabled "foot soldiers" have been used to devastating effect. They pointed to a case in February when a suicide bomber in a wheelchair killed an Iraqi general in Samarra, north of Baghdad.[229]

Returning to the case of David that was mentioned at the beginning of this section, he traveled to India where he remained in the group for just three weeks. Without medication he had a series of psychotic episodes. After being thrown out of the group, he managed to find his way back to his family in Australia, stayed with them for one night, and left early the following morning.

David was missing for two weeks when the family received a call from a psychiatric hospital announcing their son had been admitted. He had been found wandering the streets, telling everyone he met that he was the new guru of the cult. Fortunately, he was found alive and could be treated. Tragically, there are many like David who are not so fortunate.

6

The Dilemma
for Families

As I was researching the issue of radicalization by terrorist organizations and searching for some basic principles and values that might offer protection, I came across the book *My Year Inside Radical Islam* by Daveed Gartenstein-Ross. The author converted to Islam while at college out of a desire to connect to a religious community and spiritual practice but gradually found himself seduced into the most extreme and radical interpretation of Islam. His book chronicles this fascinating but disturbing journey and ends with his decision to relinquish all ties with Islam.

I found the book revealing because the author was born in the United States. He was brought up in a Jewish home and, prior to joining a terrorist organization, had his eyes on a career in law within the mainstream community.

In attempting to make sense of his experience, Gartenstein-Ross makes a poignant comment towards the end of the book.

"Part of the seduction of Islam is its otherness—how different it is from anything else. And it would be a mistake to short change how satisfying a life is inside radical Islam. As I descended into radicalism I had a greater degree of certainty than I had known before. I felt that for the first time I could truly comprehend and follow Allah's will—and I knew that those who disagreed with me were just following their own desires. There was a sense of community which came with this certainty. I was part of an exclusive club composed of those who could see beyond the shallow Western liberal values with which I was raised."[230]

Two points are highly significant: the sense of certainty and the accompanying sense of community that radical Islam offered. These are the issues that families and community leaders must address if they are to answer the question, "What can we do to safeguard our loved ones from involvement in extremist activity?"

The Role of Family and Community

"For many, the rise of the global economy marks the final fulfillment of the great dream of a global village. Almost everywhere you travel today you will find multi-lane highways, concrete cities and a cultural landscape featuring fast-food chains, Hollywood films, and cellular phones.

"The world, we are told, is being united by virtue of the fact that everyone will soon be able to indulge their innate human desire for a Westernized, urbanized consumer lifestyle. West is best and joining the bandwagon brings closer a harmonious union of peaceable, rational, democratic consumers 'like us.'

"This worldview assumes that it was the chaotic diversity of cultures, values, and beliefs that lay behind the conflicts of the past, that as these differences are removed, so the differences between people will be resolved.

"Villages, rural communities and their cultural traditions around the world are being destroyed on an unprecedented scale under the impact of globalizing market forces. Communities that have sustained themselves for hundreds of years are simply disintegrating. The spread of the consumer culture seems unstoppable."[231]

Chloe was a young woman when she became involved in a destructive therapy group. Eventually she left and sued the leaders. Later still she expressed a sense of regret for her decision to take legal action. "I still longed for the sense of community and belonging I'd felt in the group. The emotions we had experienced together were so intense that I had felt bonded with these people for life, as though we were survivors of a plane crash."[232]

The sense of community provided by cult organizations is one of their most effective tools. Former members of terrorist organizations recognize that the lure to succumb to the recruitment process was enhanced by the community nature of the whole operation, and the attractiveness of that pull cannot be underestimated.

Moreover, such an appeal has been enhanced by the diminishing strength of local communities that no longer offer the security and cohesiveness they once did. As the global community juggernaut rolls on, many people continue to have a deep yearning for a caring form of living that values the individual.

But there appears to be no going back. The virtual community through Internet sites such as MySpace, Facebook, and Twitter have become the means by which people interact and share their lives and their secrets. In truth, there is nothing special or sacred about the virtual community.

The most disturbing aspect of this phenomenon, however, is in the alienated young people who are finding homes in the hate chat rooms where they are exposed to all forms of unbridled prejudice and discrimination. According to a United Nations study, young people who access terrorist websites are often driven by a desire to connect, be engaged and identify with others who share similar interests; the sense of community offered by these websites is exciting and empowering. Many of these websites deliberately offer a sense of belonging and purpose to the individual who seeks to effect change and be part of a vision for the future. Their preoccupation with the Internet, in turn, breeds introversion and isolation from the mitigating influences of friends and family thus creating a greater vulnerability to radicalization.

Such a progression is documented in the book *The Islamist* by Ed Husain,[233] which traces the author's radicalization from an East London Muslim choirboy to an operative of the Hizb ut-Tahrir terrorist organization. Husain's ability to discover a sense of community, albeit within the dark world of terrorism, is significant.

Husain argues that the rival factions of the radical Muslim youth organizations he encountered offered "dynamism, Englishness and religiosity." He went from one to another, drawn deeper each time into extremism, and finally reached Hizb ut-Tahrir, where, he writes, "We thought we were making a new world. Our job was to mobilize the Muslim masses here. There was that feeling of being on the cusp of a new world order which would revive the glory days of Islam. For a seventeen-year-old who felt out of place in the UK, it was very attractive. Everywhere we went, we were the brothers to be respected. It was intoxicating."[234]

These opportunities for the individual who seeks meaning and excitement contrast starkly with the experience of many people in a world that is increasingly dominated by global influences. Nagaoka Hiroyuki, head of the Aum Shinri Kyo Victims' Association, was sprayed with VX nerve agent by Aum members in 1995. At the trial of one his assailants he recounted his career as a typical Japanese corporate employee, working very long hours, having limited contact with his family, and traveling from city to city. His son joined the Aum terrorist cult because he felt rootless in relation to family and school and he quit his job. When his son finally left Aum he told his father he had returned "because you have changed."

In a penetrating interview in 1997 after the Aum attacks in Tokyo, Nagaoka said, "I spent many years as a salary man. Every time I got promoted, they made me take a training session, a virtual confinement in a hotel, and when they were over, I felt I could die for the company. When I remember my feelings in those days, I can understand that people can be made to think it is right to kill."[235]

For cult members the contrast between community life within the organization and life on the outside is stark. A young member of the Heaven's Gate cult by the name of Dick Joslyn tells how he decided to leave the doomsday organization in 1979. He picked himself up and walked away from the campsite down a long road, arriving back in the earthly world as manifested in an all night truck stop near Cheyenne, Wyoming. Looking at the waitresses and the truckers chewing down breakfast, he decided that the world did not have much to offer, hitched back to the campsite the same morning, and stayed there for another fourteen years.[236]

The Value of Certainty

"Cults promote a message which claims certainty about issues which are objectively uncertain. Despite this logical flaw, the message is alluring. Most of us want to believe that the world is more orderly than it is, and that some authority figure has compelling answers to all life's problems. An individual who claims to have 'The Truth' is more convincing than someone who announces 'I don't know.'"[237]

In her book titled *The Seductiveness of Certainty: The Destruction of Islam's Intellectual Legacy by the Fundamentalists*, Tamara Albertini highlights how contemporary Muslim fundamentalists reduce Islam's rich and complex intellectual legacy to a set of authoritarian rules. This reductionist impulse eliminates both the scholarly space of inquiry and the room for individual reflection traditionally granted to its followers by Islam.

There is a seductiveness in certainty that provides comfort and solace for people seeking to find a place in an increasingly uncertain world. As this uncertainty continues to grow, so too does the lure of those organizations who preach certainty.

The growth of uncertainty is not without grounds. It is difficult to overstate the far-reaching effects of globalization, which include the internationalization of markets, the subsequent decline in national borders, and intensified competition.

A paper titled "Globalization, Uncertainty and Youth in Society," published by Globalife, a research arm of the Bamberg University, suggests that globalization creates an atmosphere of increasing uncertainty that is filtered through country-specific institutions and perceptions. "The institutions of welfare regimes, employment, education and family systems that operate during the transition to adulthood channel uncertainty to specific social groups of youth which in turn impacts their opportunity or ability to make decisions during the transition to adulthood. Yet youth are in a life course phase where they need to make vital and long-term binding decisions about entering the labor market and forming a partnership or family."[238]

The threat of climate change and concerns regarding global warming add to an uncertainty that for many youths underlies their struggle to make sense of a volatile world. Post 9/11, the world continues to face the uncertainty of terrorism and the very real possibility of further attacks at any time. The commonly expressed view—that it is not a question if there will be another major attack but when that attack will be—amplifies this sense of uncertainty.

Against this backdrop, organizations that promise an element of certainty are welcomed. One of the hallmarks of cults and fringe religious groups is their tendency to provide simple solutions in response to complex questions. The group's doctrine clearly enunciates issues of life, morality, marriage, money, and work.

For the terrorist, much of the world's complexity is irrelevant. For the suicide bomber, climate change has no meaning. The only significance of globalization lies in the dream that one day sharia law will become a global phenomenon.

It follows that the feeling of a haven offered by cults or terrorist organizations should not be underestimated. These organizations offer emotional, physical, financial, spiritual, and existential security. The member is led to believe that he has friends and family on whom he can rely unconditionally. At the same time the organizational doctrine of the cult or terrorist organization spells out the meaning and purpose of the member's life.[239]

Dennis Tourish, co-author of the book *On the Edge: Political Cults, Right and Left*, writes, "The world becomes divided into the absolutely good and the absolutely evil, a black and white universe in which there is only ever the one right way to think, feel and behave. Members are immunized against doubt—a mental state in which any behavior is possible, providing it is ordained by a leader to whom they have entrusted their now blunted moral sensibilities."

7

Responding to Cults—A Role for Governments and Lawmakers

In 2007 a Sydney woman was charged with the murder of her father and teenage sister. According to an article in the *Sydney Morning Herald*, in a submission to the court the clinical director of Liverpool and Fairfield Mental Health Services, solicitor Mark Cross, said that the woman had been diagnosed with a psychiatric illness late last year, but follow-up from Bankstown Hospital's mental health team had apparently been declined by her parents owing to "their alleged Scientology beliefs." She had told him her parents did not want her to take her prescribed drugs.

But a spokeswoman for Scientology is reported to have said that she doubted the family belonged to the church. It had no knowledge of them and had never had contact with them.[240]

What Scientology doesn't deny is their rejection of psychiatry and psychiatric drugs. Scientology doesn't deny that two years ago celebrity actor, Tom Cruise shouted down the U.S. television presenter Matt Lauer for daring to suggest that pharmaceuticals might sometimes help treat psychological disorders.[241]

I have always found the issue of civil liberties and the right to free speech is particularly perplexing in relation to cults and extremist groups. Civil libertarians have raised major moral and ethical issues regarding a range of issues including security, censorship, human rights, and free speech. Meanwhile, the public is often left confounded about the applications of these principles. Should, for example, a church be permitted to espouse its vehemently negative views about psychiatry or medicine to a vulnerable audience made up of people who may be in need of specialist care?

Several years ago I was invited to address a group of a hundred or more former members of the Exclusive Brethren. The vast majority of attendees were people whose partners and children were still in the church but who had no access to them because of alleged decrees of excommunication. Considering that the Exclusive Brethren are often parents of large families, I figured that somewhere in Australia there could have been close to a thousand children who no longer had any contact whatsoever with one or both parents.

Some time later I read the comments of a judge of the Australian Court in relation to the admission by a woman that she would not allow her children to see a photograph of their father who was no longer in the church. "How sad it was that this house was so poisonous to the father that they could not even have a photograph of the father in their home."[242]

Several questions need to be asked: At what point does a government have the right to intervene in order to protect members of the public from alleged abuse at the hands of a cult or terrorist organization? Are the ages of the alleged victims relevant considering the coercive processes and mind control techniques often used by these groups? What recourse do individuals and families have to fight back against individuals or organizations whose rights to spread spurious messages of poisonous seduction are protected?

Although the following sections focus on some of the contentious issues facing the judiciary and the government in dealing with cults, many of the issues raised are equally relevant in relation to terrorist organizations. The debate continues regarding whether counter terrorism laws represent a threat to political freedom, civil liberties, and constitutional rights. In Australia in a 2002 Melbourne University Law Review titled "'Counter-Terrorism' Laws: A Threat To Political Freedom, Civil Liberties And Constitutional Rights," the author, Michael Head, wrote, "The events of September 11 have been utilised to bring forward unprecedented measures that will substantially expand the powers of the security agencies. Both the context of the legislation, and the extraordinary reach of its measures, invite constitutional challenge as well as public opposition."[243] In the USA, Amnesty International voiced its concerns about alleged breaches of human rights following the 9/11 attacks.[244] Similar concerns were echoed in other countries.[245]

And at the same time, some families of terrorists have argued that their loved ones were brainwashed into adopting a murderous ideology and should not be treated by the courts as criminals. If the process of radicalization orchestrated by terrorist organizations does indeed involve a process of brainwashing or indoctrination, do governments have a responsibility to intervene to stop this process?

Cults, Civil Liberties, and Religious Freedom

"Freedom of religion is not freedom, for example, to defraud, nor is it freedom to cause significant psychological or psychiatric harm to any person."[246]

"What is happening in Texas since the court ordered the evacuation of children from the polygamist enclave known as the Fundamentalist Church of Jesus Christ of Latter Day Saints is mind-boggling, so unreal on so many levels, so heartbreaking. Almost eerily so, both sides question how this could happen in modern-day America.

"Merril Jessop, who oversees the ranch, told the Salt Lake Tribune: *'There needs to be a public outcry that goes far and wide... The hauling off of women and children matches anything in Russia or Germany.' The mothers who have returned to the compound are shown crying. 'It's like Hitler,' one said. 'How can this happen in America? This is religious persecution.'*

"But, then, you see glimpses of the young girls in their identical ankle-length, hand-sewn dresses, their hair—forbidden ever to be cut—worn up in elaborate braids. Some as young as 13 and 14 appear very pregnant. Others carry infants."[247]

The manner by which cults should be treated in the hands of governments and the law is controversial because it touches upon our basic notions about freedom of religion. Any attempts to curtail the operation of a religious group are bound to attract criticism from civil libertarian organizations as well as from a wary public concerned about the misuse of public control.

Ironically, cults often accuse authorities of intolerance and religious vilification. Exit counselors are accused of brainwashing their clients and denying them their basic religious rights.

Caught in the middle is the family who seeks assistance through legal or other means to re-establish contact with a loved one. While there are some avenues to pursue allegations of physical and sexual abuse, few options exist in regard to psychological or emotional manipulation and abuse.

When the Australian Government decided to withdraw seventy-two children from the Children of God in 1993, various civil liberty groups leapt to the group's defense, and eventually the children were returned to the communes from which they had been removed.

In Japan, Aum Shinri Kyo, which was responsible for the sarin attacks on the Tokyo subway system in 1995, has regrouped and continues to grow. Although the cult was outlawed in Russia, Japanese authorities have been reluctant to invoke a 1952 anti-subversive law that would ban the group, citing concerns for civil liberties and religious freedom.

At the same time, people who oppose cults also invoke the issue of civil liberties. In a speech to the Australian Parliament, Steven Mutch, MP, said, "I believe the community has a right to know what occurs in destructive cults, and I intend to continue exposing the practices of this particular cult until people ... find freedom from a very real and very dangerous mind control. To me it is a fundamental question of civil liberties."[248]

Also in Australia, Prime Minister Kevin Rudd rejected the pleas of former members of the Exclusive Brethren for a broad-ranging inquiry into the sect, saying such an investigation would "unreasonably interfere" with their right "to practice their faith freely and openly."

The request for an enquiry had been prompted by a letter written by a former member of the Brethren, Peter Flinn, and signed by thirty-three others in which they highlighted the "disproportionately high taxpayer funding of Brethren schools, dishonest political campaigning, their charitable status in relation to rate and tax exemptions, and their well-known intimidatory tactics during traumatic Family Court cases."[249]

As journalist Shakira Hussein has written, "Religious freedom requires that religious groups are allowed to practice their faith, but it should also provide their members with exit routes. At the moment, the Exclusive Brethren do not provide such exits—and government funding, particularly of the Brethren schools, enables them to maintain this closure." [250]

In May 2008, an anti-Scientology protester was issued a summons by the City of London Police for refusing to remove his sign reading: Scientology is not a religion, it is a dangerous cult.

Subsequently the police dropped the charges against the protestor for using the word cult in a move the human rights group Liberty called a free speech victory.

Liberty's legal director, James Welch, who was advising the young man, said, "At last an outbreak of common sense; but pretty worrying for free speech that the police even threatened this young man with prosecution."[251]

There is no question that the notions of freedom of speech and religion are embedded in the constitutions of most western democracies. However, there is ample documentation to show that there are vulnerable members of society who may be unduly influenced by groups that are not totally honest or transparent regarding their mission. Because cults and various fringe churches in particular may appeal to a more fragile section of society, civil libertarians need to be conscious of the fact that in attempting to protect the rights of people, they may be exposing them to undue influences with potentially dangerous ramifications.

Cults and Courts

In May 2008, state police arrested the leader of an apocalyptic sect in north eastern New Mexico. Sixty-six-year-old Wayne Bent was charged with three counts of criminal sexual contact with a minor and three counts of contributing to the delinquency of a minor.

According to the affidavit for the arrest warrant, Bent was accused of touching three girls in 2006 and 2007. All of them were under eighteen at the time, and one of them was twelve. Bent, who goes by the name of Michael Travesser and claims to be the Messiah, is the leader of The Lord Our Righteousness Church, whose members moved in 2000 to a remote, former ranch near the Colorado line.[252]

While many cults have been accused of breaking the law, responses by the authorities are limited to specific offenses and not the general operation or influence of the particular group. These offenses usually relate to tax matters, corporate reporting requirements, and violation of immigration laws. There are numerous examples of successful court prosecutions of cult leaders.

In 1982, Sun Myung Moon, divine leader of the Unification Church, was convicted in the United States of tax fraud and sentenced to an eighteen month jail term and a $15,000 fine. He served thirteen months of the sentence at a minimum-security prison and because of good behavior was released to a halfway house before returning home.

In 1985, Bhagwan Shree Rajneesh (later called Osho), pleaded guilty to immigration fraud and was deported from the United States. He was refused entry by twenty-one countries and eventually settled in Puna, India.

In 1994, after a lengthy trial, Shoko Asahara, the leader of Aum Shinri Kyo, which orchestrated the sarin gas attacks on the Tokyo subway system, was sentenced to death. Eleven other members of the group were also sentenced to death.

In 2002, the Chiba District Court in Japan sentenced Koji Takahashi, leader of the Life Space, cult to fifteen years in prison for murdering a sixty-six-year-old man whose mummified body was found at a hotel in Chiba Prefecture.

In 2005, in Australia, William Kamm, also known as the Little Pebble, was convicted of molesting a fifteen-year-old girl and was sentenced to five years in prison. Kamm claimed that the victim was one of his eighty-four mystical wives. In 2007, Kamm was found guilty of aggravated sexual assault and aggravated indecent assault in relation to another teenage girl. The sexual relationship had continued from the time the girl was fourteen until she was nineteen, when she became pregnant and gave birth to his child. In August 2007, after having lost an appeal on his earlier sentence, Kamm faced a maximum ten years in jail with a seven-and-a-half-year non-parole period.[253]

In June 2008, a Russian court handed down a two year suspended prison sentence to the leader of Toward God's Kingdom who was found guilty of forming an extremist group and inciting ethnic hatred in the Astrakhan district near Russia's southern border with Georgia.

Whereas these judgments are relatively straightforward, judgments relating to cult leaders who have caused psychological or emotional damage to children are more complex and difficult to substantiate. Assessment of the damage is far more difficult to quantify as is the level of culpability of an individual.

In response to this issue, an Australian government committee has recommended that "significant emotional harm" inflicted by religious groups be classified as a criminal offense. A government report cited a California Supreme Court finding that "coercive persuasion" by religious sects could cause "serious physical and psychiatric disorders."[254]

The committee named the techniques used by cults as isolation, manipulation of time and attention, positive and negative reinforcement, peer group pressure, prohibition of dissent, deprivation of sleep and protein, and the inducement of fear, guilt, and emotional dependence.

Significantly, courts have recognized that a court-appointed child's representative in a cult-related case could facilitate an assessment of the child's mental state and the influence of the group on the child. In some cases this has led to a court making specific rulings to protect the child, or, in more extreme cases, removing the child from the cult environment.[255] The use of an expert witness's testimony has also been of particular assistance to courts seeking to make a ruling in a cult-related family matter.

In February 2007, in the Family Court of Australia, Justice Robert Benjamingave three members of an Exclusive Brethren family, including the respondent mother, suspended jail sentences for denying a father access to two of his children in contravention of orders of the court.

The judgment was an emphatic statement by the Family Court that it would not tolerate the Exclusive Brethren continuing to flout court orders in pursuit of the sect's policy of strict separation of its members from those who have left the church.

"What happened in this case is that the court said to these people, 'Do not breach these orders,' in circumstances where the finding was clear that the separation of the children and their father was at the higher end of emotional abuse," Justice Benjamin said. "I made it absolutely clear. Yet some two or three weeks later, a breach occurred. In this case a term of imprisonment is entirely appropriate."

Justice Benjamin concluded that the family had put pressure on the children not to go on the visit. "These children are entitled to have a relationship with their father, and the steps that the respondents have taken to prevent the relationship are extraordinary and poor."[256]

In relation to adult cult members, the situation is quite different. Police cannot respond to complaints lodged by parents unless it can be demonstrated that an offense has been committed by the cult. There is very limited recourse for parents who are concerned about the plight of their adult children involved in a cult, regardless of the effects. Even when there are grounds for legal action by former members of a cult—for example a breach of a duty of care—such a course can be expensive and traumatic.

Former members of cults have attempted to recover funds that were voluntarily handed over to their leaders. In some situations, the cult leaders have chosen to settle the claim for fear of public exposure. In other situations, the claimants have attempted to argue that there was a breach of a duty of care on the part of the leaders.

When called upon in such cases, it is crucial for courts to understand the influence that cults exercise over their following. In relation to the Exclusive Brethren, psychologist Louise Samways said that many in the Family Court system did not understand the "ferocity of the fear planted in these children" by fundamentalist sects such as the Brethren. Samways said that the organization taught that people outside were condemned to hell and that association with outsiders would cost members their salvation. [257]

On July 5, 2007, the sentences handed down by Justice Ben¬jamin in the above case, were set aside on appeal to the Full Court of the Family Court. The court did not then rule on the sanction to be imposed on the mother. On September 13, 2007 the Full Court required the mother to make a contribution towards the father's costs, but imposed no other penalty

In a further application, on June 25, 2009 Justice Sally Brown granted the mother sole parental responsibility for the children and discharged all orders requiring them to spend time or communicate with their father. Her Honour said that "I cannot find any positive benefit to the children in making orders which require them to spend time with their father; nor any prospect of them having a meaningful relationship with him in the forseeable future." Justice Brown's views on the Brethren were generally positive: their religious conviction was as "vital as the air they breathe." A court-appointed consultant suggested that contact between the father and his two children should occur for "an hour or two, once or twice a year." However, Justice Brown said that she could not see any benefit in that. Instead, the father at his own expense could be provided with a copy of their school reports, photos and newsletters as long as he obtained them at a time when any family members "are not likely to be on the school premises."

Controversial cases such as this one further underscore the need for the judiciary to understand the issue of cultism and mind control. For many families, the courts represent the only opportunity to protect a loved one from the influence of a cult, a fringe church, or an extremist group.

Government Intervention

"Internet sites and blogs which peddle the gospel of an 'anorexic lifestyle' to teenage girls were outlawed by the French parliament yesterday. The law is the first attempt anywhere in the world to stamp out the 'Pro-Ana' movement, a cult-like attempt to promote anorexia as a lifestyle which began in the United States eight years ago."[258]

Although governments throughout the world have been successful in regulating or closing down the operation of suspect individuals whose practice is alleged to include cult-like techniques, their responses to larger, more established cults has been ineffective.

Perhaps the most famous example of government intervention relates to the roles of the FBI and ATF in the Waco disaster in February 1993 in which seventy-four people including twenty-one children perished in the fire that engulfed David Koresh's commune in Texas. In their book *Why Waco?*, authors James D. Tabor and Eugene V. Gallagher argue that the situation could have been handled differently and possibly resolved peacefully. "This is not unfounded speculation or wishful thinking. It is the considered opinion of the lawyers who spent the most time with the Davidians during the siege and of various scholars of religion who understand biblical apocalyptic belief systems such as that of the Branch Davidians. There was a way to communicate with these biblically oriented people, but it had nothing to do with hostage rescue or counterterrorist tactics."[259]

In Australia the 1993 raid of the Children of God communes and the forced removal of seventy-two children was a failure. Within a week the children were returned to the commune. Subsequent investigations found that the Department of Community Service that authorized the operation was ill-informed and acted beyond its legal capacity.

The statute of limitations prevented the Australian authorities from prosecuting Anne Hamilton-Byrne for the harm and suffering she caused to the children whom she had reared in the draconian cult environment she created. The victims of Hamilton-Byrne's cruelty were outraged when they found out that the only offenses with which she could be charged related to frauds involving false birth certificates and passports. Survivors found it difficult to accept that there was never going to be any form of retribution for all the years of abuse.

In the United States, the forced removal of 489 children from the Fundamentalist Church of Jesus Christ of Latter Day Saints, a breakaway group from the Mormon Church, was also short lived. The decision by the local authorities to remove the children was based on allegations of underage sex, rape, and forced marriages between minors and elders of the church. Two months later the Texas Supreme Court ruled that the removal of the children was illegal, and they had to be returned due to lack of evidence that they were being abused.

Even where the authorities are successful in closing down a cult, the group is able to restart their operations using a different name. This was the case in Australia in 2002 where a particular group, Infinity Forms of Yellow Remember, was closed down by the NSW Department Fair Trading Commission. The organization was targeted for marketing its products as miracle cures though the products were allegedly simply distilled water with exotic names like Heart Spider and Puff the Magic Dragon. Within weeks of being shut down it was alleged that the group was operating again under the name Hermes Far Eastern Shining.[260]

Elsewhere, governments have tried to make cults illegal. According to the Catholic Newsagency, in November 2007 the interior ministers of Germany's sixteen states launched an investigation into the activities of the Church of Scientology, hoping to ban the U.S.-based organization from operating in Germany. The promoter of the initiative, Udo Nagel, said that Scientology was incompatible with the German constitution and called it a "psycho-sect" seeking "the absolute repression of the individual."[261]

But skeptics questioned whether such a move was politically and legally tenable, or wise. An earlier 1997 move by the state-level interior ministers concluded in its report that "the Scientology organization, agenda and activities are marked by objectives that are fundamentally and permanently directed at abolishing the free democratic basic order, but that more time was needed to 'conclusively evaluate' the group."[262]

The history of government intervention in cult-related matters reveals a string of relatively ineffective steps to shut down groups or to remove members of an organization who are thought to be at risk. Essentially, governments have lacked an understanding of the nature of cultism and mind control. There is also a poor record of governments working with professional organizations that actually understand cult dynamics.

Government Controls

"Our modern community and church-based organizations do have to have a separation of church and state—they do not proselytize religion, it is not part of their professional practice. Prayer is not a medical treatment."[263]

"They tell you your true friends will get in the business, support your being in the business and/or buy your (Amway) products. There's a lot of hero worship, a lot of earning people's friendship. You get to go to people's homes and to their parties based on what you accomplish, not based on who you are. They have very charismatic speakers with a lot of energy. It's not a business, it's a community. They provide you with family, love and friendship. They feed you ideas on religion, politics and relationships. They tell you everything about how to act and how to think."[264]

Despite the difficulties involved in attempting to introduce controls into the booming phenomenon of cults and cult-like personal development groups, the matter deserves urgent attention. Such groups operate without any form of accreditation, often awarding certificates or diplomas of no recognized academic or professional value. Many of these groups purport to offer salvation and healing to vulnerable and often desperate individuals. Exorbitant sums of money are extracted with little or no return to the member. Likewise, fringe churches assume the mantle of established religious organizations without revealing their true identity or disclosing their long-term agendas while spiritualists and psychic healers are able to practice without any formal training or external control.

The issue of regulating multi-level marketing groups came under scrutiny in 2007 when the British government attempted to close down the British subsidiary of Amway. For many years the world-wide Amway network has been the target of accusations that it operates as a cult. In her book *Dangerous Persuaders*, Australian psychologist Louise Samways wrote that increasingly Amway is adopting similar tactics to many cults in order to attract recruits and then to keep them involved and committed. At extremely large gatherings techniques used by traditional cults are employed to reinforce values and enhance commitment.

The case brought by the British government against Amway included claims that the promise of wealth was illusory and amounted to nothing more than a dream. Mark Cunningham QC, representing the government, said that Amway presented itself to be life changing and life enhancing. "We will show you otherwise," he said. He argued that in 2005 and 2006 there were 39,000 Amway agents in Britain but 71 percent of them earned nothing while 90 percent of the agents had experienced a loss after paying the fee to renew their registration. In May 2008, however, the judges dismissed the claim after noting that the radical changes introduced by the company had remedied the earlier faults.[265]

Many such failures would be avoided were it possible to educate government and non-government personnel regarding cults and their subtle processes of psychological manipulation and mind control. This information is relevant to numerous agencies, including the family courts, departments of community and human services, child abuse and protective agencies, sexual abuse clinics, medical practitioners, and counseling services.

The challenge for governments and lawmakers is to put in place a code of ethics under a regulatory board that can oversee their operation. Failure to do so should attract appropriate penalties as well as the possibility of the organization being closed down.

In addition, programs for mental health professionals could assist them in understanding the specific nature of cult behavior. The sudden disappearance of a cult member from a clos-knit family or what appears to be the adoption of a new personality can lead to frustration on the part of these professionals who may be tempted to diagnose the behavior using more conventional models. According to Paul Martin, who has written extensively on the subject, such clients are frequently misdiagnosed as suffering from a bipolar or psychotic disorder because their traumatic symptoms may mimic these conditions.

To date governments and lawmakers have been mainly reactive regarding cult issues. A mass suicide or the disappearance of an individual into a cult tends to mobilize the relevant authorities into suggesting new laws or controls for these groups, but as quickly as concerns arise, they dissipate. Families and communities deserve better. The vast majorities of communities pride themselves for their tolerance and the freedom of their members. If the beneficiaries of this freedom are destructive cults and fringe churches, then the way these principles are being applied in our society must be examined.

8

Responding to
the Terrorist
Threat

The tallest building in my Australian hometown of Melbourne is the Rialto. In fact, it actually consists of two towers and often reminds me of the Twin Towers that once dominated the Manhattan skyline. Shortly after September 11, 2001, I paid a visit to the city with my two youngest children.

As we drove past the towers my then six-year-old child asked his older brother, "When the terrorists blow up that building, which building will be the tallest one in Melbourne?" The question stunned me and made me wonder how these innocent young children see life in a post-9/11 world.

We have become so used to terrorism; it is simply another part of the political and social landscape. The term suicide bomber has become commonplace, and we have become desensitized to images of mangled buses and flying body parts. In doing so, we have cheapened the value of life. A terrorist attack with a single digit death toll hardly rates a mention.

Our acceptance of this new form of warfare, which specifically targets civilians, and in some situations children, suggests a sense of resignation implying that we have lost the war. We have also accepted the process of radicalization and the frightening influence of terrorist organizations. This is nothing short of a global tragedy. The manner in which governments and lawmakers respond to the global terrorist threat would be, arguably, the biggest challenge facing them today. The catastrophic damage caused by these organizations and their implications are huge.

Meanwhile, governments, churches, political leaders, and research organizations continue to look for effective responses. The former secretary of the United Nations, Kofi Annan, has sketched out a plan based on five "D"s: dissuade disaffected groups from choosing terrorism as a tactic to achieve their goals; deny terrorists the means to carry out their attacks; deter states from supporting terrorists; develop state capacity to prevent terrorism; and defend human rights in the struggle against terrorism.[266]

Gareth Evans, president of the International Crisis Group, has suggested a strategy in slightly more operational terms based on five "P"s: a protection strategy; a policing strategy; a political strategy; a peace building strategy; and a psychological strategy.[267]

Though a comprehensive discussion regarding these models is beyond the scope of this book, the issues of mind control and how they impact on the war on terror is certainly relevant. In this light I would like to suggest another model in terms of the five "M"s that underlie the substance of terrorist recruitment: mind control, manipulation, misinterpretation, martyrdom, and marginalization. One of the fundamental challenges today is to find the means by which to address these dynamics.

Mind Control and Manipulation

"Something felt different this time, though. Before, I felt lost walking through the park - feeling that I needed to think about something, but unable to pinpoint what it was. It was as though my time as an Islamic fundamentalist had dulled me, stripping me of the ability to think for myself."[268]

"Last July, the British government unveiled an $18 million de-radicalization program aimed at tackling Islamist extremism at the local level. The London-based Quilliam Foundation, which was founded by former members of the radical Islamic organiza-

tion Hizb ut-Tahrir (Party of Liberation), is one part of that effort. Quilliam promotes a version of Islam that is compatible with Western democratic values and rejects the notion promoted by groups such as the Muslim Brotherhood and Al Qaeda, which say Muslims must create a state governed by Islamic law, or Shariah, wherever they live. In many respects, Quilliam practices a form of cult prevention: In this case, the cult is a political ideology that distorts the Islamic faith.[269]

At a seminar titled "Genocide and Terrorism: Probing the Mind of the Perpetrator," Juan Cole, President of the Global Americana Institute, presented a paper titled "Al Qaeda's Doomsday Document and Psychological Manipulation"[270] on the mind of the 9/11 terrorists. His comments are significant in that they highlight the connection between mind control and terrorism not only in terms of the processes of recruitment and radicalization but also in relation to the execution of an actual terrorist attack.

Cole argued that the internal psychology of commitment to murder on a huge scale and to die in the process was underpinned by an almost obsessive-compulsive immersion in the details of repeated rituals. Reciting sacred phrases with every activity, the internal monologue of the terrorists was drowned in a set of sacred mantras, leaving no space for questioning orders.

Cole suggested that the constant hum of recitation is a tool used by terrorist organizations to introduce a liminal state, which is not entirely conscious but forms an important part of the training process. The intensity and lack of small talk amongst the hijackers probably derived from their silent, constant dhikr or repetition of sacred verses. This liminal consciousness may have been reinforced by deliberate sleep deprivation and by bouts of drunkenness. Cole concludes, "Employed as they were intended, the techniques of Islamic mysticism have produced saints and sages like Rumi and al-Ghazali. Misused as a form of brainwashing, they appear to have contributed to some of the largest mass murders in history."[271]

Numerous accounts of terrorist activities point to the radical-ization process that transforms the ideologue to the murderer and the peace activist to the assassin. In each of these situations the need to understand the process of mind control is paramount.

The stories of young people who return from a brief visit to Af-ghanistan or Pakistan having taken up arms for a terrorist cause are familiar. Governments, lawmakers, and community leaders can no longer sit still. Quite apart from the expansive list of measures that are being taken to contain and control terrorism, the importance of preventative measures cannot be overstated. Four steps are worth mentioning.

1. Educational Programs

Educational institutions can and should teach students about mind control and other psychologically invasive practices. In relation to physical and emotional safety, schools around the world have adopted protective behavior programs that aim to enhance the problem-solving and communication skills of people of all ages. These programs encourage individuals to identify situations that are unsafe, or potentially unsafe, and to develop strategies to coun-ter threats and preserve their physical and emotional safety. These programs could be extended to address the dangers of mind control. Programs that teach students about these invasive and dangerous processes would enable them to be better prepared to resist some of the insidious methods used by terrorist organizations to recruit and radicalize young people.

Currently the International Cultic Studies Association (ICSA) oversees a number of preventive education activities that are or-ganized under the International Cult Education Program. These programs are available to clergy, educators, and others interested in teaching young people critical-thinking skills so they can resist un-ethical sales techniques, peer pressure, and other forms of psycho-logical manipulation. While the emphasis of these programs is on recruitment by cults, fringe churches, multi-level marketing agencies, and personal development groups, they need to be extended to include the psychologically manipulative techniques used by terrorist organizations in recruiting and radicalizing their members.

2. Mentoring Programs

Community leaders should explore various models for mentoring programs that link minority individuals with successful members of mainstream society. According to Susie Kay, President and Founder of the Hoops Dream Scholarship Fund, by forming relationships with at-risk youths, mentors and advisors who might otherwise not have any contact with troubled communities are able to gain an understanding of the challenges facing these youth. Conversely, young people can learn some of the necessary skills and habits of educational success from their mainstream mentors.

Healthy mentoring programs also have the potential to neutralize the impact of charismatic leaders whose dynamism serves as a powerful agent in the recruitment of young people in search of directions. The increasing acceptability and use of mentoring programs is encouraging. The challenge for communities is to implement these programs in the areas where they are needed most.

One area where mentoring can play a significant role is the prison system, which has been recognized as fertile territory for recruitment. While re-education programs for terrorists have met with success, more work is required to prevent inmates who have no prior association with terrorists from being swept in by the terrorist agenda. Many terrorists, including the notorious shoe bomber Richard Ried, were recruited in prisons.[272]

3. Civic Engagement

Government institutions, clergy, and community leaders can all assist young people in finding opportunities for civic engagement in community-based service groups, sports activities, arts and literary groups, and more formal activism such as voting and political engagement. Such opportunities assist young people in defining their identities in a manner beneficial to themselves and to society.[273]

Bearing in mind that the search for identity and the desire to belong are fundamental needs of adolescents, civic engagement can be seen as a direct antidote to the vulnerability that is exploited by terrorist organizations, which, if harnessed correctly, should be seen as an important part of any program to combat the recruitment and radicalization of young people

4. Law Enforcement and Intelligence

Law enforcement and intelligence agencies need to familiarize themselves with the complex phenomena of mind control and the means by which young people are radicalized. Steve Hassan comments, "We should be using our knowledge of mind control psychology to undermine the control and power of the people on top of the pyramid of this and other terrorist organizations."[274]

Benjamin Zablocki, professor of sociology at Rutgers University, has advocated the need for governments to be pro-active in learning about the tactics that are used to push vulnerable individuals into carrying out acts of violence. "Society doesn't really know what it is that they're dealing with, they don't really understand this force and the potency of the force. It's enormously effective in changing the individual and creating what is known as a deployable agent, who will do anything that he or she is told to do."[275]

Governments would be serving their constituents well if they would be prepared to fund research projects aimed at studying, among other things, the factors that drive young people towards association with terrorist groups, what makes some young people more vulnerable, and the personal needs and hopes that are addressed by such groups.

Misinterpretation and Martyrdom

> *"Islamic terrorism is the divine duty of pure Muslims for which they feel pride instead of feeling remorse. Pure Muslims do not call it terrorism they only call it Islamic Jihad against the infidel west. Killing non-Muslims are sacred duty of every devout Muslim for which Allah repeatedly commanded (in Qur'an) and declared unlimited reward in the after life. Muslims those who read Qur'an and understand it well always believe in the Islamic 'global agenda' that Islam has a sacred and mandatory God given duty to spread Islamic message (Din-e-Islam) to all the inhabitants of the world."*[276]
>
> *"A passionate desire for martyrdom and death does not come about as a natural consequence of anger or frustration. Children and their parents are indoctrinated through controlled television, religious sermons, school textbooks, and other media sources, to believe that martyrdom is a religious and patriotic obligation, and is rewarded by an afterlife of eternal bliss. They live surrounded in an environment that glorifies the shahid. Martyrs' pictures hang on walls in homes, mosques and schools, and appear, like those of celebrities, on television."*[277]

Following 9/11 former world heavyweight boxing champion Muhammad Ali at a telethon benefit concert for the victims of the terrorist attacks said, "I'm a Muslim. I've been a Muslim for 20 years. I want the world to know the truth about Islam. I wouldn't be here to represent Islam if it were the way the terrorists make it look ... Islam is for peace."[278]

Shaykh Abdul Aziz al-Ashaikh, Grand Mufti of Saudi Arabia and Chairman of the Senior Ulama, added his voice to the chorus of Moslem leaders around the world on September 15, 2001:"Hijacking planes, terrorizing innocent people and shedding blood constitute a form of injustice that can not be tolerated by Islam, which views them as gross crimes and sinful acts."[279]

A record of similar statements by high-ranking international Muslim scholars and leaders appeared in an advertisement placed by the Becket Fund for Religious Liberty in the *New York Times* on October 17, 2001.[280]

Despite these efforts, attacks around the world continue to wreak havoc, create misery, and destabilize communities. Numerous Imams and other Islamic clerics continue to preach hatred while the number of young people lining up to become suicide bombers continues to grow.

Considering that propaganda is one of the more effective tools of mind control, it is logical to assume that neutralizing terrorist propaganda would be a significant starting point in the war against terror. Since not only leaders of the Islamic faith but leaders of other religions accept that it is a misinterpretation of Islamic teachings that has led to the scourge of terrorism and the cult of martyrdom, the need for corrective information could not be more urgent.

A number of options present themselves: deconstructing the jihadist propaganda and exposing the flaws within their material; effective education programs; government controls, and censorship of hate material; anti-terrorism media campaigns. Finally, the proactive involvement of Islamic leaders in correcting the terrorists' misinterpretation of Islam is pivotal in any attempt to curtail and eventually eradicating Islamic fundamentalist terrorism.

According to Cheryl Benard, the deconstruction of jihadist propaganda is an effective means to counter this misinterpretation of Islam. Tactics include dispelling the impression that volunteers are honored and valued for their violent acts, that they have made a considered and free decision, and that their families and the general population agree with their acts and venerate them.

"Instead one can demonstrate that ordinary Moslem families and communities are repulsed by these acts; that the suicide bomber was not chosen because he is so cherished by his group but because they consider him expendable; that many do not go to their deaths freely but are tricked or pressured into doing so; that their acts cause not jubilation but suffering on the part of ordinary families."[281]

Young people should be informed about the risks involved in terrorist activity and the possibility that they may spend the remainder of their lives in prison. They will eventually be forgotten by their families and will remain outcasts of society. Benard argues that anything that encourages a reasoned decision rather than an impulsive act should be encouraged.

Although there have been many suggestions about controlling the use of the Internet, many experts argue that attempts to shut down terrorist websites would be of limited value as there are many means to get around such restrictions. It is not merely a question of civil liberties. Rather, they argue, shutting down offending Internet sites, as the European Union has suggested, is short-sighted and of limited value.

More significantly, the Internet can be exploited by intelligence agencies by using counter-propaganda to deconstruct the myths of martyrdom and the misinterpretation of Islam. It has also been suggested that the West do more to encourage moderate Islam to better engage in the online debate and to assert more visibly its place vis-à-vis the extremists who, after all, represent only a small faction in Islamic cyber-space.[282]

The ability to neutralize extremist Islamic views rests also with effective educational programs that emphasize fundamental human rights and generate respect for others while conveying skills for creating and maintaining cultures of peace. Textbooks need to be reviewed by the relevant government authorities so that hate material and radical agendas are prohibited. Extremist ideologies that exploit grievances and twist religious beliefs need to be exposed for what they are.

Moreover, an education agenda should not be limited to school curricula. Schools and other educational systems need to focus on the culture in which children are reared and educated and how this culture impacts on their lives. In most of the world, streets, public buildings, and schools are named after presidents, great musicians, scientists, and others who might serve as role models for children. However, Palestinian towns such as Yaabid named their most important street and schools after former Iraqi dictator Saddam Hussein.[283] One of the numerous examples of schools named after terrorists is the Dalal Mughrabi School, which honors the man who killed American photographer Gail Rubin and thirty-six Israelis.[284] Before the children open a book, they already know who is to be emulated.

Governments need to extend their efforts to control and censor the distribution of hate material. Nevertheless, despite much rhetoric about protecting vulnerable people from the messages of hate that are being spewed out by terrorist organizations, this issue remains controversial. This issue was put to the test in Australia in early 2007 when Australian Federal Police raided a number of stores in Sydney seizing various materials that appeared to promote terrorism. One such item included a series of pro-terror hate DVDs that urged children to martyr themselves in Islam's war on the West. The film called for the murder of non-believers.

In one DVD, the Australian-born radical Sheik Feiz, now in exile in Lebanon, blamed a lack of courage for martyrdom on the battlefield for the "humiliation" of Muslims in Iraq, Afghanistan, Palestine, and Guantánamo. The film, one of ten in a series titled *The Death Series*, urged parents to make their children holy warriors and martyrs, and praises Jihad as the pinnacle of Islam.

However, in a decision that was strongly criticized by numerous experts in terrorism, the Australian Office of Film and Literature Classification (OFLC) ruled that *The Death Series* was suitable to be bought and watched by children. The finding meant that children of any age could watch the films, but advised parental consent for those under fifteen. In fact, the decision came as the sheikh was allegedly still preaching to Australians by phone. The OFLC finding said the sheik's calls to Jihad and martyrdom were ambiguous. It also found that comments vilifying Jews as an "army of pigs" and saying "behind me is a Jew, come kill him" were mitigated by the context.[285]

In other arenas there have been calls for an anti-terrorism media campaign to counter the Islamist propaganda disseminated through various news agencies including Al-Jazeera. Some media experts have argued that terrorist groups have adopted the media in efforts at psychological warfare to both recruit terrorists and demoralize, confuse, and suborn their victims. "The western media has shown itself once again to be the Islamists' most powerful weapon against the free world on what few realize is the real battleground of the free mind."[286]

In an article published by the Middle East Media Research Institute, Amine Allami, a columnist for the Algerian daily *Liberté*, wrote, "In order to counter this daily media attack by the terrorists it is necessary and even urgent, to launch a new anti-terrorism media campaign."

In the *Liberté* editorial, Allami reiterated the need to counter jihadist propaganda, writing, "It is inconceivable that we should stand idly by while the Al Qaeda propaganda machine disseminates misinformation and falsehood, with the help of Al-Jazeera and other Middle Eastern media outlets and websites, and manipulates young Algerians in order to recruit them for terrorist activities."[287]

Finally, the role of Islamic authorities and spiritual leaders in promoting the view that terrorism represents a gross misinterpretation of Islamic teachings continues to demand attention. It has been suggested that Muslim communities, particularly in Europe, often lack credible spokespeople to advance a moderate message.[288]

A powerful example of the contentious nature of this issue was the November 2007 fatwa denouncing terrorists and their violence issued by the Fique Council of North America, a leading Islamic authority in North America. The fatwa stated its unequivocal and unqualified condemnation of the destruction and violence committed against innocent men and women.

"This condemnation of violence is deeply rooted in true Islamic values based on the Koran's instructions which consider the unjust killing of a single person equivalent to the killing of all humanity (Koran 5:32). There is no justification in Islam for extremism or terrorism.

"Targeting civilians' life and property through suicide bombings or any other method of attack is prohibited in Islam—*haram*—and those who commit these barbaric acts are criminals, not 'martyrs.'"[289]

The fatwa was met with strong criticism. The fatwa condemned violence against "innocent men and women," but because jihadists contend that no non-Muslim is innocent, a jihadist who reads this fatwa could agree with it entirely and continue to carry out violent attacks against those he considered to be *buffer harbi*—infidels at war with Islam, and not innocents at all. The failure of the Fique Council to define what is meant by "innocent men and women" was viewed as a significant flaw in the fatwa.

The tragedy is that while all these issues are being discussed, the glorification of martyrdom continues. One powerful video clip, shown regularly on Palestine Authority–controlled TV during the past three years, shows a schoolboy writing a farewell letter to his parents. "Do not be sad, my dear mother, and do not cry over my parting, my dear father. For my country, I shall sacrifice myself." The child leaves home and joins his friends in a riot. He places himself in front of the soldiers, is shot in the chest, and collapses. The words are sung, "How sweet is martyrdom when I embrace you, my land," as he falls to the ground embracing the land. As the boy's mother is seen crying, the letter continues, "My beloved, my mother, my most dear, be joyous over my blood and do not cry for me." The message is clear, it should be the goal of every Palestinian child to join the cult of martyrdom.[290]

It was Abu Qaqa al-Tamimi's nine-year-old son who said to his father, "Daddy, I want to be a martyr. Can you get me an explosive belt?" In response, he told his little boy that he was too young to become a martyr. Nevertheless, he says he taught the nine-year-old how to make roadside bombs and how to fashion a rudimentary rocket launcher out of metal tubes. "We have to prepare the next generation for battle. We have to realize that the fight against the Americans might last a long, long time."[291]

Marginalization

"Exclusion based on ethnic origin, religion or national origin is often compounded by political, as well as economic and social exclusion. On the social and economic side, particular attention should be paid to youth unemployment. Globally, young people are three times as likely to be unemployed as adults. In some countries youth unemployment rates remain entrenched and of worrying proportions. Taken together these various types of exclusion can combine to produce a volatile mix. Marginalization, alienation and the resulting sense of victimization can propel extremism, which can in turn facilitate exploitation by terrorists."[292]

In an essay based on encounters with extremist youth and their families called "An Arsenal of Believers," in the *New Yorker* in 2001, Nasra Hassan offers an explanation for the motives behind terrorism. She offers the experience of indignities suffered, of political humiliation, and of desperation borne out of a sense of futility, as possible explanations of why some people turn to terror.[293]

Research supports the argument that marginalization and alienation will increase a young person's desire to search for status and identity and to belong. Unemployment and the fact that young people are often deprived of any constructive outlet for their time and energies are also relevant and contribute to vulnerability.[294]

In 2005, it was estimated that in the San Fernando Valley area of Los Angeles there were seventy active street gangs with a membership of over 15,000 young people.[295] Numerous researchers have identified the desire to belong as one of the fundamental reasons why young marginalized and alienated people join street gangs.

One writer summed up the street gang phenomena on a blog: "Some people do some pretty extreme things to be accepted by others. Street Gangs—chilling gang rituals: slashing defenseless strangers, breaking buddies' bones, raping and murdering innocent girls—these are rights of passage for many teenagers looking towards gang culture for a sense of belonging."[296]

In explaining what led him to embrace terrorism, Ed Husain describes a febrile culture in Britain in the early 1990s when studious Muslim second-generation teenagers felt dislocated both from the country in which they lived and from their parents. Husain found himself drifting away from the pious Sufi Islam of his parents to their horror. "I was looking for somewhere to fit in. We were exposed to white working-class culture and it wasn't comfortable. We may have been poor, but we had middle class values—psychologically, I felt out of place."[297]

The issue of marginalization is complex and has far-reaching implications. Although young people may feel that their position in society has been compromised because of a particular injustice, there is the possibility that the aggrieved person will move beyond his own situation and identify with broader, more global causes of injustice or unfairness. This was the experience in Iraq after the second Iraq war when it became clear that numerous splinter terrorist groups joined forces with Al Qaeda in an effort to defeat U.S. forces.

This point was articulated in a speech by the Dutch Prime Minister, Jan Peter Balkenende, in 2003, in which he stated that societies must promote political and economic freedom in order to remain innovative and competitive. "If they don't, differences in relative wealth and modernity will be catalysts of envy and friction." Mr. Balkenende highlighted the significant risks to Dutch society, when feelings of injustice and despair develop into solidarity with a "broader struggle".

Mr Balkenende also urged countries to address the issue of alienation from a rapidly changing world as a major cause of terrorism. "Rapid development puts high demands on the ability of communities and people to adapt. Not being able to cope with a changing environment can cause distress and insecurity. This can alienate people from the societies they live in."

The Prime Minister said that in changing situations, people look for familiar anchors to cling on to. He said that although religion, culture, and traditions could provide stability, in the hands of extremists they would become a tool for radicalization, hatred and resistance to change. "Closed groups that do not fully participate in our society are vulnerable to extremism." [298]

The connection between marginalization and the propensity for extremism emerged as a major national crisis during the race riots that ravaged Paris in November 2005. The rioting over a period of two weeks left more than six thousand cars burned, public and private property destroyed, tens of policemen injured, and one civilian dead.

The unrest was blamed on social and economic marginalization of the African and Muslim immigrants in the European country. One former union activist said, "There will be no solution to the crisis in the near future unless the government changes its policies toward marginalized immigrants."[299] The activist urged the French parliament to debate the root causes of crisis, describing the unrest as "a revolution by desperate youths who have lost all hopes." [300]

The underlying issues of the Paris riots were reflected in a July 2007 paper, "Addressing Youth Radicalization in the Mediterranean Region," which highlighted youth unemployment and social marginalization as empirical facts that had to be taken into account in dealing with Muslim communities in Europe. The paper argued that this sense of economic and social marginalization made certain members of migrant communities more susceptible to the narrative of violent extremists. In particular, unemployment can lead to alienation, with one of the possible outcomes, participation in a terrorist network.

The paper argues that taking steps to address unemployment, particularly among youth migrant communities in Europe where rates are high, should be an essential part of counter-terrorism strategies. "Young people in these migrant communities need to be made to feel more connected to the broader European society and be given more employment opportunities to help them to move away from the disturbing trend of creating parallel societies."[301]

Prime Minister Balkenende summed up the challenges associated with issues of marginalization and alienation when he commented that although there is no easy way to solve the problem of terrorism, the need to integrate people and to provide them with equal opportunities is a significant part of the struggle. At a global level he called for a sense of community between nations, saying, "We need to be open and ready to assist each other. In openness and dialogue we can find out what unites us rather than what divides us."[302]

Epilogue

In the 1960s it was difficult to imagine that a few, relatively new Eastern cults would be the forerunners of what has been termed an epidemic of sudden personality change. Even in 1978, the tragedy of Jonestown seemed an isolated incident.

Similarly, the term suicide bomber was unfamiliar. When the first suicide bombers occurred in the 1970s the world was shocked. Today, suicide bombings are seen as a standard albeit malignant feature of the contemporary word, a kind of social virus like HIV. As the world continues to experience the harsh reality and implications of cults and terrorism, the issue of mind control has become crucial to understanding these phenomena.

In regard to cults, there is little room for optimism. New groups are mushrooming, and though these new groups present a far more professional image, they are no less dangerous.

While governments attempt to balance the demands of the anti-cult movement against civil libertarians, cult activity is able to continue unabated. And while particular tragedies create an outpouring of emotion and a call for change, these sentiments are usually short-lived.

In my home country of Australia, geographical isolation and government apathy have enabled numerous cults to establish themselves. The specific cases highlighted in this book demonstrate a government approach which has been either ineffective or misguided.

In Australia Section 116 of the Constitution, and in the United States the First Amendment, have provided a safety zone within which the cults can operate, though this was probably not the intention of the founding fathers or the authors of the constitutions. Other Western countries offer similar tolerance through which the cults are given a free hand. There is little reason and even less hope for change in the short term.

If cults are a challenge to society at large, then there is a particular responsibility on the part of the churches to respond aggressively and effectively. Although it is becoming increasingly clear that cults are not simply a religious issue, it is also clear that their attraction is often couched in religious or spiritual terms.

While the events of 9/11—and the frightening increase in terrorism since that time - have pressured communities to confront the issues of cultism and mind control, experts argue that without a deeper understanding of the processes and techniques used by terrorist organizations, there is little hope that their activities can be curtailed.

Tragically, there is every reason that the war on terror is a long-term proposition. As fundamentalism becomes more entrenched in society, and individualism is stifled by the implications of globalization, young people will seek opportunities to belong. In an increasingly dangerous and fragile world an involvement in terrorism appears less bizarre.

At the same time, until governments are able to find the means to control the unfettered dissemination of hate material, many young people will develop worldviews within a framework of prejudice, hatred, and violence. And until governments and communities can address the alienation of marginalized youth, their communities will continue to harbor ticking time bombs ready to ignite without warning.

On a global scale, terrorist organizations are now so adept at using the Internet to recruit, indoctrinate, and communicate that intelligence experts talk about the emergence of a terrorist "sanctuary in cyberspace."[303] One terrorist expert has suggested that 80 percent of the recruitment of youths by terrorist organizations is now achieved via the Internet. "These groups now avoid using old tactics, such as meeting in mosques; they now meet in cafes and sports clubs."[304]

A report in July 2008 by the London-based Center for Social Cohesion entitled, "Islam on Campus: A Survey of UK Student Opinion," showed that 32 percent of Muslim students said killing in the name of religion could be justified, while 60 percent of active members of on-campus Islamic societies said the same. "These findings are deeply alarming," said Hannah Stuart, one of the report's authors. "Students in higher education are the future leaders of their communities. Yet significant numbers of them appear to hold beliefs which contravene liberal, democratic values." Stuart added, "In addition, there are signs of growing religious segregation on campus. These results are deeply embarrassing for those who have said there is no extremism in British universities," she said.[305]

At the same time Islamic leaders lament the damage that terrorism has perpetrated on their faith. According to Ahmad Syafii Maarif, an Indonesian peace activist, "The terrorists hijack God. Their theology is the theology of death. Terrorism has defaced Islam and given it a bad name. We have to go deep into the authenticity of religion. Religion has a moral message. Justice is the key to global wisdom, and without it, the world will go astray forever."[306]

Ultimately, cultism and terrorism have exposed the frailty and vulnerability of the human mind. They have shown that we are far from immune to the carefully contrived plans of groups and organizations that well understand the notion of mind control and psychological manipulation. What was once regarded as a phenomenon unique to prisoners of war and hostages is now seen as a major threat to personal autonomy, individuality, and ultimately to our freedom as citizens.

Young people are particularly vulnerable to the influence of cults and terrorist organizations. As David Canter writes, "There seems to be a stage in life—particularly late teens, early twenties—where individuals are trying to seek out their identity. They're trying to understand what sort of person they are and of what significance they are going to be in the world. Often, these individuals, for a while anyway, go through a period where they see commitment to some sort of ideal as a way of giving meaning or identity to their lives. And it is this search for an ideal that makes them vulnerable to people offering them these extreme, radical solutions."[307]

We have learnt the extent of our vulnerability as we compare the techniques used by the Third Reich with those of some of the more extreme cults that we face today.

In her book *Seductive Poison*, Deborah Layton documents her escape from Jonestown and her attempt to alert the world of the impending carnage. Deborah's mother died in that attack. Her brother, Larry, was imprisoned for over twenty years having been implicated in the murder of Congressman Leo Ryan and other dignitaries who had gone to Jonestown to investigate the cult.

Layton's words provide a fitting conclusion to this work:

"When our thoughts are forbidden, when our questions are not allowed and our doubts are punished, when contacts and friendships outside of the organization are censored, we are being abused for an end which never justifies the means. When our heart aches knowing we have made friendships and secret attachments which will be forever forbidden if we leave, we are in danger. When we consider staying in a group because we cannot bear the loss, disappointment and sorrow our leaving will cause for ourselves and those we have come to love, we are in a cult.

"If there is any lesson to be learnt it is that an ideal can never be brought about by fear, abuse, and the threat of retribution. When family and friends are used as a weapon in order to force us to stay in an organization, something has gone terribly wrong. If I, as a young woman, had had someone explain to me what cults are and how indoctrination works, my story might not have been the same."

Appendix
The Doomsday Document

Mohammed Atta is alleged to have been the mastermind of the 9/11 terror attacks on the United States. It is believed that he flew American Airlines Flight 11 into the first tower of the World Trade Center. Left behind in his luggage was a four-page handwritten document that has become known as the "Doomsday Document."

The translation below is by Juan Cole, President of the Global Americana Institute.

The Last Night

1. Vow to accept death, renew admonition of the base self, shave the extra hair on the body, perfume yourself, and ritually wash yourself.

2. Know the plan well from every angle. Anticipate the reaction or the resistance of the enemy.

3. Read the surahs of Repentance and The Spoils. Contemplate their meaning and the bounties God has prepared and established for the martyrs.

4. Remind your base self to listen and obey this night, for you will be exposed to decisive turning points wherein listening and obey-

ing is one hundred percent necessary. Train your base self, make it understand, convince it, and goad it on to this end. "And obey God, and His Messenger, and do not quarrel together, and so lose heart, and your power depart; and be patient; surely God is with the patient."

5. Staying up at night and imploring in prayer for victory and strength and perspicuous triumph, and the easing of our task, and concealment.

6. Much recitation of sacred phrases. Know that the best of dhikr is reciting the noble Qur'an. This is the consensus of the people of knowledge or, indeed, of the most learned. It is enough for us that it is the words of the creator of the heavens and the earth toward Whom you are advancing.

7. Purify your heart and cleanse it of stains. Forget and be oblivious to that thing called the world. For the time for playing has passed, and the time has arrived for the rendezvous with the eternal Truth. How much of our lives we have wasted! Shall we not take advantage of these hours to offer up acts of nearness [to God] and obedience?

8. Let your breast be filled with gladness, for there is nothing between you and your wedding but mere seconds. Thereby will begin a happy and contented life and immortal blessing with the prophets, the true ones and the righteous martyrs. They are the best of companions. We beseech God for his grace. So seek good omens. For the Prophet, may blessings and peace be upon him, used to love divination about every matter.

9. Then fix your gaze, such that if you fall into tribulations, you will know how to behave, how to stand firm, how to say "We are, verily, from God and to him we shall return." Thus you will know that

what has befallen you is not because of any error you committed. That you committed an error was not so that you would face tribulations. That calamity of yours is in fact from God, may he be exalted and glorified—so as to elevate your station and cause your sins to be forgiven. Know that it is only a matter of seconds before it shines forth by the permission of God. Then blessed is he who attains the great recompense from God. God says, "Did you think you would enter paradise when God knows those who strove among you, and knows the patient?" "Am hasabtum an tadkhulu al-jannat . . ."

10. Then recite (tadhkharu) the words of God, "You were wishing for death before you encountered it, then you saw it, and are looking for it . . ." And you wanted it. After that, recite the verse "Kam min fi'ah qalilah ghalaba fi'ah kathirah bi idhn Allah . . ." And In yunsirukum Allah fa la ghalib lakum . . ."

11. Bring your base self, as well as your brethren, to remembrance through prayers. And contemplate their meaning, recitations (adhkar) of morning and evening, recitations of city (baldah), recitations of . . .(makan), recitations of meeting (liqa' al-Tur) . . .

12. The jet: with breath (an-nafs), suitcase, clothing, knife, tools, identity papers, passport and all your papers.

13. Inspect your weapon before setting out and before you even begin to set out and "Let every one of you sharpen his knife and kill his animal (dhabiha) and bring about comfort and relief of his slaughter" before the journey.

14. Pull your clothes tightly about you, for this is the way of the pious ancestors (as-salaf as-salih), may God be pleased with them. They pulled their clothing tightly about them before a battle. Pull your shoelaces tight and wear tight socks that grip the shoes and do not come out of them. All of these are means that we have been

commanded to adopt. God has hasabna and he is the best of advocates (na'im al-wakil).

15. Pray the morning prayers in congregation and reflect on the reward for doing so while you are performing recitation afterwards. Do not go out of your apartment without having performed ablutions. For the angels seek forgiveness for you as long as you have prepared ablutions and they pray on your behalf.

Notes

Introduction

1. *FACTnet Newsletter*, January 2002.
2. Aron, Raphael, *Cults: Too Good To Be True* Melbourne, Australia. Harper Collins, 1999.
3. For the purpose of this book, the terms mind control, thought reform and brainwashing were used interchangeably.
4. The attack on the Ma'alot school in Israel in October 1974 also appears to have targeted children.
5. Statement by cult expert Steve Hassan, following the attacks of September 11, 200,1 published on his website, www.freedomofmind.com/stevehassan/presskit/releases/09-11-01.htm.
6. Statement by cult expert Steve Hassan, September 20, 2001, published on his website, www.freedomofmind.com/stevehassan/presskit/releases/09-20-01.htm.
7. NMHA News Releases, September 17, 2001; February 15, 2002.
8. AAP, October 2001.
9. Conway, Flo and Jim Sigelman. *Snapping: America's Epidemic of Sudden Personality Change.* New York: Stillpoint Press, 1978 (updated 1995, second edition).

Chapter One

10. "Common Myths about al Qaeda Terrorism." *E-journal USA*, September 2006.
11. "Implementing the UN General Assembly's Counter-Terrorism Strategy: Addressing Youth Radicalisation in the Mediterranean Region. Lessons Learned, Best Practices and Recommendations." The Istituto Affari Internazionali (IAI) and the Center for Global Counter Terrorism Co-operation.

Rome, July 11-12, 2007.

12. Lorenz, Konrad. *Australia Israel Review*, May 1978.

13. Rudin, Marcia. "Cults Not Gone, Just Mainstreaming." *The Cult Observer* (1993): Vol. 10, No. 10.

14. In December 2004 *American Family Foundation* officially changed its name to International Cultic Studies Association (ICSA).

15. "The Departed Children." *The Province*, Vancouver, 1989.

16. Ross, Rick. "The Tate LaBianca Murders and the Manson Family." www.culteducation.com.

17. "Bioterrorism is Next Big Threat, Expert Warns." *The Oregonian*, March 11, 1998. See also Torok ,Thomas J., MD, et al., *Journal of the American Medical Association* (1997): 278:389-395.

18. Layaco, Richard. "The Lure of the Cults." *Time*, April 1997.

19. *Delaware County Times*, August 1989.

20. "Doomsday Destructive Cults: The Order of the Solar Temple." About.com: Alternative Religions.

21. Kaplan, David E. and Andrew Marshall. *The Cult at the End of the World The Terrifying Story of the Aum Doomsday Cult*. New York: Crown, 1996. See also "Hearings Before the Permanent Subcommittee on Investigations of the Committee on Governmental Affairs, United States Senate," (October 21 and November 1, 1995): Part I.

22. Gleik, Elizabeth. "The Marker We've Been Waiting For." *Time*, April 1997.

23. *The Herald Sun,* July 1997.

24. Fisher, Ian. "Ugandan Villagers Avoiding Cult Massacre Site." *The New York Times,* July 6, 2000.

25. Mowak, David. "Last Members Leave Penza Cave." *St. Petersburg Times,* May 20, 2008.

26. Norrie, Justin. "Explosion of Cults in Japan Fails to Heal Deadly Past." *The Melbourne Age*, November 2007.

27. ZKEA Biological Welfare, Biological Terrorism, Emerging Diseases. "Religion and Biological Terrorism." www.zkea.com/archives/archive01003.html.

28. Terrorism Recovery Imapact. Harvard Program in Refugee Trauma, Department of Psychiatry, Massachusetts General Hospital.

29. Dodd, Scott and Peter Smolowitz. *The Deseret News*, October 2003.

30. Kach, Kahane Chai (Israel extremists). The Council on Foreign Relations, New York, March 2008.

31. www.terrorism-research.com.

32. "Religion and Terrorism: Interview with Bruce Hoffman." *Religioscope,* January 2002.

33. National Counterterrorism Center, Annex of Statistical Information, US Department of State, April 2007.

34. "Transnational Terrorism: The Threat to Australia." Australian Government Department of Foreign Affairs and Trade, 2004.

35. Snow, Robert L., "Deadly Cults: The Crimes of True Believers." Westport, CT: Greenwood Pub. Group, 2003.

36. Wolf, Christopher. "Regulating Hate Speech Qua Speech Is Not the Solution to the Epidemic of Hate on the Internet." Paper presented at OSCE meeting on the Relationship Between Racist, Xenophobic and Anti-Semitic Propaganda on the Internet and Hate Crimes, Paris, France, June, 16-17, 2004.

37. For example: Twelve Tribes at www.twelvetribes.com The Unification Church at www.unification.org; Hare Krishna at www.harekrishna.com; Sai Baba at www.sthysai.org; Osho at www.osho.com.

38. Carr-Greg, Dr. Michael. Letter to the Editor, "The Dangers of Love Bombing." *The Melbourne Age*, April 1997, Melbourne, Australia.

39. Snow, Robert L. "Deadly Cults: The Crimes of True Believers." Westport, CT: Greenwood Pub. Group, 2003.

40. Sang-Min Whang Leo, Sujin Lee, Geunyoung Chang. "CyberPsychology & Behavior Internet Over-Users' Psychological Profiles: A Behavior Sampling Analysis on Internet Addiction." *CyberPsychology & Behavior* (April 1, 2003): 6 (2): 143-150.

41. Weimann, Gabriel. "How Modern Terrorism Uses the Internet." United States Institute for Peace. March 2006.

42. Verton, Dan. "Black Ice: The Invisible Threat of CyberTerrorism." Columbus, Ohio: McGraw-Hill/Osborne, 2003.

43. Weimann, Gabriel. "How Modern Terrorism Uses the Internet." United States Institute for Peace. March 2006.

44. For example: www.ex-cult.org provides general support for former members from a variety of organizations. www.escapeint.org provides support for former members of the Church of Scientology; www.silentlambs.org provides support for former members of the Jehovah's Witnesses; http://lessonsinawareness.com/intro.aspx provides support to former members of Training in Power, a personal development group based in Seattle, Washington.

45. Warne, Dan. "Anonymous Threatens to 'dismantle' Church of Scientology via Internet." *APC*, January 2008.

46. Lemost, Robert. "Safety: Assessing the Infrastructure Risk."   Cnet news.com, August 2002.

Chapter Two

47. Friscolanti, Michael, Jonathan Gatehouse and Charlie Gillis with Nicholas Kohler, Colin Campbell and Luiza Ch. Savage. "Homegrown Terrorist Attack Thwarted." *McLeans Magazine*, June 2006.

48. Zablocki, Benjamin. "The Blacklisting of a Concept. The Strange His-

tory of the Brainwashing Conjecture in the Sociology of Religion." *Nova Religio: The Journal of Alternative and Emergent Religions* (October, 1997): vol. 1, n. 1 , pp. 96-121.

49. Zimbardo, Phillip. "Mind Control: Psychological Reality or Mindless Rhetoric." *Cultic Studies Review* (2002): Vol. 1, No. 3.

50. Ibid.

51. Singer, Margaret Thaler. *The Cult Observer* (1994): Vol. 11, No. 6.

52. Ibid.

53. "Al-Qaeda Terrorist Selection and Recruitment." The Rand Corporation National Security Research Division.

54. Ibid.

55. Rotella, Sebastian. "Social Bonds Pull Muslim Youth to Jihad, Expert Says." *Los Angeles Times*, October 2004.

56. Sageman, Marc. *Understanding Terror Networks*. Pennsylvania: University of Pennsylvania Press, 2004.

57. Interview with CBC, May 3, 2007.

58. Lifton, Robert J. "Cult Formation." *The Harvard Mental Health Letter* (February 1991): Vol. 7, No. 8.

59. Ibid. See also Singer, Margaret with Janja Lalich, *Cults in Our Midst*. San Francisco: Jossey-Bass, CA, 1996.

60. Brett, Cate. "History of the Exclusive Brethren." *North South,* New Zealand, March 1993.

61. Bell, Rachel. "'Willing to Die,' Palestinian Suicide Bombers." TruTV Crime Library, 2006.

62. Singer, Margaret with Janja Lilich. *Cults in our Midst*. San Francisco: Jossey-Boss, CA 1996. For an excellent article on the use of language by cults see Ye Lahua, Professor Institute of Religious Studies, Shanghai Academy of Social Sciences, "On the Spiritual Manipulation of the Cult." Paper presented at the International Forum on Cultic Studies (Shenzhen) and sponsored by the Center for the Study of Destructive Cults, Chinese Academy of Social Sciences, Shenzhen, China, January 2009.

63. Cole, Juan. "Al-Qaeda's Doomsday Document and Psychological Manipulation." Paper presented at Genocide and Terrorism: Probing the Mind of the Perpetrator, Yale Center for Genocide Studies, New Haven, April 2003.

64. "The Apocalypse has been Postponed." *The Independent on Sunday,* May 1995.

65. "The World: A Passion to Know the End is Nigh." *New York Times,* October 1994.

66. "Most Cults Share Similar Attributes." *Zwire*, October 2001.

67. Richardson, Louise. *What Terrorists Want: Understanding the Enemy, Containing the Threat.* New York: Random House, 2006.

68. A Case Study of the Terrorist Cult of Mojahedin-e Khalq; the Nejat

Association.

69. Heftman, Erica. *WCCO-TV*, Minneapolis, Minnesota, 1980.

70. "Osama bin Laden's Media Director Puts on a Show at Guantanamo." *The Huffington Post*, May 2008.

71. Van Leen W.A (ed.). "'O is for Orange'—An Examination of the Rajneesh religion, also Known as the Orange People." Perth, Western Australia: Concerned Christian Growth Ministries Inc., 1982.

72. Robert Baer, a former CIA field officer assigned to the Middle East.

73. Samraj, Adi Da. *I Have Come for the Sake of all Beings; An Introduction to Adi Da and his Wisdom-Teaching. California.* USA: The Dawn Horse Press for the Free Daist Avataric Communion, 1995.

74. Kelly, Bulkeley, Ph.D. Graduate Theological Union in Berkeley, California.

75. Whyche, Stephanie L. "The Cult of Terrorism." *Intelihealth News Service*.

76. Lithwick, Dahlia. "The Brainwashed Defence: Will Walker's, Moussaoui's and Ried's Lawyers Breathe New Life into an Old Tactic?" *Slate Magazine*, January 2002.

77. Hamilton-Byrne, Sarah. *Unseen, Unheard, Unknown.* Victoria, Australia: Penguin Books Australia, 1995.

78. Whyche, Stephanie L. "The Cult of Terrorism." *Intelihealth News Service*.

79. Snow, Robert L. *Deadly Cults: The Crimes of True Believers.* Westport, CT: Greenwood Publishing Group, 2003.

80. Ghosh, Bobby. "Inside the Mind of an Iraqi Suicide Bomber." *Time Magazine*, June 2005.

81. Dossey, Larry. *Recovering the Soul.*

82. Columnist Abdallah Rashidin writing in the United Arab Emirates daily *Al-Itihad* on the issue of Iraqi terrorism. UJA Federation of Greater Toronto.

83. "Last Members Leave Penza Cave." *The St Petersburg Times*, May 2008.

84. "Brussels Calls for Media Code to Avoid Aiding Terrorists." *Guardian. co.uk.* September 2005.

85. The University of Texas at Austin. Interview with Dr Ami Pedahzur www.utexas.edu/features/2006/terrorism/index.html.

86. *The Detroit News*, April 2008.

87. "Jewish Reporter Meets Want-to-be Bomber." *YNet News.com*, November 2006.

88. Hassan, Steven. *Combatting Cult Mind Control.* Rochester, Vt.: Park Street Press, 1990.

89. Langone, Michael. *Recovery From Cults.* United States: W.W. Norton & Company, 1995.

90. West, L.J. Paper presented at the American Family Foundation Con-

ference, Arlington, VA, May 1992.

91. *The Harvard Mental Health Letter.* (February 1981): Vol. 7, No. 8.

92. Lewin, Kurt. "Frontiers in Group Dynamics: Concept, Method and Reality in Social Science; Social Equilibria and Social Change." *Human Relations* (1947): Vol. 1, No. 1 5-42.

93. Lithwick Dahlia. "The Brainwashed Defence: Will Walker's, Moussaoui's and Ried's Lawyers Breathe New Life into an Old Tactic?" *Slate Magazine*, January, 2002.

94. Liberty Think, December 2003. www.libertythink.com.

95. www.rickross.com/groups/attleboro.html.

96. California appellate court, 2nd district, 7th division, Wollersheim v. Church of Scientology of California, Civ. No. B023193 Cal. Super (1986).

97. "Scientology pays $8,674,643 to ex-member to end 22-year legal battle." *FACTnet Newsletter,* May 2002. www.factnet.org/letters/FACTNews-May2002Wollersheim.html.

98. Kokkinakus v. Greece (14307/88) [1993] ECHR 20 (25 May, 1993).

99. "Man's Brother Talks of Brainwashing." *48 Hours CBS,* October 4, 2001.

100. *New York Times*, January 2002.

101. *FACTnet Newsletter*, January 2002.

Chapter Three

102. Herdy, Amy and Robert Farley. "Bin Laden Was his Hero, But Who Was his Friend?" *St. Petersburg Times,* February 2002.

103. Senputa, Kim. "The Lonelinesss of the Child Suicide Bomber." *The New Zealand Herald,* June 2008.

104. Yoder, Vincent Cyrus, Thomas B. Virden III, Kiran Amin. "Internet Pornography and Loneliness: An Association?" *Sexual Addiction & Compulsivity* (2005): Volume: 12 Issue: 1.

105. Zimbardo, Dr. Philip. *The American Psychological Association Monitor*, May 1997.

106. Daly, Rich. "Don't Look For Mental Illness to Explain Terrorist Acts." *Psychiatry News*, July 20, 2007.

107. Hamilton-Byrne, Sarah. *Unseen, Unheard, Unknown.* Victoria, Australia: Penguin Books Australia, 1995.

108. Chisholm, Patricia with Suvendrini Kakuchi. "Japanese Cult Leader Arrested." *MacLean's Magazine*, May 1995.

109. The University of Texas at Austin. Interview with Dr Ami Pedahzur.

110. Lorenz, Konrad, quoted in Australia Israel Review, May 1978.

111. Whyche, Stephanie L. "The Cult of Terrorism," *Intelihealth News Service.*

112. Ibid.

113. Layton, Deborah. *Seductive Poison*. California: Random House, 1998.

114. Garden, Mary. *The Serpent Rising, A Journal of Spiritual Seduction*, Australia: Brolga Publishing, 1988.

115. Salhani, Claude. "Who Are Today's Terrorists?" *Middle East Times*. May 2009.

116. Rosedale Herbert L. and Michael D. Langone, "How Many Jonestowns Will it Take?" *The Cult Observer* (1993); Vol. 10, No. 4.

117. 'est' (Erhard Training Seminars) refers to a personal development organization founded in the United States by Werner Erhard (born Jack Rosenberg) in 1971. It is regarded as the forerunner to various personal development groups operating today.

118. Financial Action Task Force, FATF-OECD, February 2008.

119. Elliot, Susan. "Is Scientology a Cult?" *Associated Centent*, February 2009.

120. Hornery, Andrew. "See ya Tom: Packer Quits Cruise's Church." *The Sydney Morning Herald*, May 2008.

121. Schlussel, Debbie. "Angelina Jolie and Oliver Stone's Terrorist Problem," debbieschlussel.com December 2004.

122. Zimbardo, Phillip. *The Lucifer Effect: Understanding How Good People Turn Evil*. New York: Random House, March 2007.

123. Affidavit of Deborah Layton Blakey. June 15 1978. www.rickross.com/reference/jonestown/jonestown12.html.

124. Statement by Islamic Society of North America (ISNA), May 2002.

125. Singer, Margaret with Janja Lalich. *Cults in Our Midst*. San Francisco: Jossey Bass, CA, 1996.

126. Reiterman, Tim, and John Jacobs. *Raven: The Untold Story of Rev. Jim Jones and His People*. United States: Dutton Adult, 1982

127. "Terrorists Are Made, Not Born: Creating Terrorists Using Social Psychological Conditioning," *Journal of Homeland Security*, March 2004.

128. Ibid.

129. Yeakley, Flavil R., *The Disciplining Dilemma*, Nashville, Tennessee: Gospel Advocate Press, 1982 as cited in Steven Hassan, *Combating Mind Control*, Park Street Press, Rochester, VT, 1990.

130. Cuthbertson, Ian M. "Terrorism and Religion, "USA." *Family Security Matters Archives*, 2006.

131. Pape, Robert. *Dying to Win: The Strategic Logic of Suicide Terrorism*. New York: Random House, 2005.

132. For a comprehensive discussion regarding this issue see *The Middle East Quarterly*, (Winter 2008): Vol. XV: No. 1.

133. "In God's Name? Evaluating the Links between Religious Extremism and Terrorism." *The Pew Forum on Religion and Public Life* (October 2005): Washington, D.C.

Chapter Four

134. Associated Press. "Layton Convicted for Role in 1978 Jonestown Killing." *Boston Globe,* December 2, 1986.

135. Elder, Miriam. "Goths Arrested on Suspicion of Murdering and Eating Teenagers in Satanic Ritual." *Telegraph.co.uk.,* September 15, 2008.

136. Fisher, Ian. "An Exhibit on Campus Celebrates Grisly Deed." *The New York Times,* Sept. 25, 2001.

137. kerenmalki.org.

138. Martin, Paul. "Seminar Compares Terrorist Groups to Cults." *Newsnet5.com,* October 2001.

139. "Social and Psychological Control." (2001): *Cult Observer,* Vol. 18, No. 04.

140. Burke, Jason, Antony Barnett, Martin Bright, Mark Townsend, Tariq Panja, and Tony Thompson. "Three Cities, Four Killers." *The Observer,* July 17, 2007.

141. Long, James. "Cults, Terrorist Groups Share Chilling Similarities, Experts Say." *The Oregonian,* November 9, 2001.

142. Bloggers, Nejat. "Mujahedin-e-Khalq as a Religious Political Cult." www.pars-iran.com. February 2009.

143. Ibid.

144. Produced and directed by David Batty and Kevin Toolis. The Disinformation Company, New York: 2004.

145. AAP. "Terrorist Reprogram Plan Torture." *The Melbourne Age,* March 2006.

146. Ibid.

147. Boucek, Christopher. "Extremist Reeducation and Rehabilitation in Saudi Arabia." *Terrorism Monitor,* (August 2007): Vol. 5, Issue 16, published by the Jamestown Foundation. It should be noted that participants in the counseling program are only terrorist sympathizers, and at the most individuals caught with jihadi propaganda. They are not individuals that have been active in terrorist violence in the kingdom; people "with blood on their hands" are barred from participating.

148. Stahelski, Anthony Ph. D. "Terrorists Are Made, Not Born: Creating Terrorists Using Social Psychological Conditioning," *Journal of Homeland Security,* Arlington VA, March 2004.

149. Cole, Juan. "Al-Qaeda's Doomsday Document and Psychological Manipulation." Paper presented at "Genocide and Terrorism: Probing the Mind of the Perpetrator," Yale Center for Genocide Studies, New Haven, April 2003.

150. "Friends Describe Bomber's Political, Religious Evolution." *washingtonpost.com,* July 2005.

151. Herbert, Ian and Kim Sengupta. "The Jihadist who Needed no Brainwashing to Blow up the Aldgate Train." *The Independent*, September 10, 2005.

152. Krueger, Alan B. "What Makes a Terrorist: Economics and the Roots of Terrorism," *Wilson Quarterly*. New Jersey: Princeton University Press, 2008.

153. Sageman, Dr. M. *Understanding Terror Networks. Pennsylvania*: University of Pennsylvania Press, 2004.

154. National Bureau of Economic Research, July 2002.

155. Hassan, Steven. *Releasing the Bonds: Empowering People to Think for Themselves*. Somerville, MA: FOM Press, 2000.

156. Van Natta, Don Jr. and Desmond Butler Ondon. "Anger on Iraq Seen as New Qaeda Recruiting Tool." *New York Times*, March 16, 2003.

157. Goolsbee, Austan. "Even for Shoe Bombers, Education and Success Are Linked." *New York Times*, September 14, 2006.

158. Ibid.

159. McCauley, Clark R. "The Psychology of Terrorism." *The Social Science Research Council*, New York, 2001.

160. Long, David E. *The Anatomy of Terrorism*, New York: Free Press, 1990.

161. Interview with CBC, May 3, 2007.

162. McCauley, Clark R. "The Psychology of Terrorism." *The Social Science Research Council*, New York, 2001.

163. Nasuti, Guy. "The Hitler Youth: An Effective Organization for Total War." militaryhistoryonline.com, 2006.

164. Clark, David. "Seminar Compares Terrorist Groups to Cults." *Newsnet5.com*, October 2001.

165. Kater, Michael H. *Hitler Youth*. Cambridge: Harvard University Press, 2004.

166. Nasuti, Guy. "The Hitler Youth: An Effective Organization for Total War." militaryhistoryonline.com, 2006.

167. Zimbardo, Phillip. *The Lucifer Effect: Understanding How Good People Turn Evil*. New York: Random House, March 2007.

168. "Christian Identity and Christian America, Hate and Violence on the Religious Right." About.com.

169. Barkun, Michael. *Religion and the Racist Right: The Origins of the Christian Identity Movement*. Chapel Hill, NC: University of North Carolina Press, 1996.

170. Tourish, Dennis Dr. and Tim Wolforth. "Prophets of the Apocalypse: White Supremacy and the Theology of Christian Identity." rickross.com, 2001.

171. Southern Poverty Law Center. Intelligence Report, Summer 1998.

172. Tuft, Carolyn and Joe Holleman. "Inside the Christian Identity Move-

ment." *St. Louis Post-Dispatch*, March 5, 2000.

173. Ahrens, Frank. "Steered to Extremism at Early Age." *The Washington Post*, June 2003.

174. Minges, Patrick. "Realized Eschatology of the Christian Identity Movement." Paper presented at the American Academy of Religion Conference, Atlanta ,Georgia, 1994.

Chapter Five

175. Layton, Deborah. *Seductive Poison*. California: Random House, 1998.

176. Corney, Peter and Kevin Giles. "Exclusivism and The Gospel." St.Hilary's Anglican Church, Kew, Victoria 1997.

177. Zukeran, Pat. "Abusive Churches: Leaving Them Behind." Probe Ministries, Texas: 1993.

178. *The Watchtower*. Vol. 116, No. 8, 6, http://www.caic.org.au/jws/control/cultic1.htm#IsReligious.

179. Jews for Jesus website. http://www.caic.org.au/jws/control/cultic1.htm#IsReligious.

180. Cited on Cult Awareness and Information Center website.

181. McDermott, Quentin. "Separate Lives." *ABC Four Corners*, September 2006.

182. Jones, Wayne. "Preacher Falls from Grace." *The Herald Sun*, December 1993.

183. Ibid.

184. Martin, Paul R. *Cult Proofing Your Kids*. Michigan: Zondervan,1993.

185. *The Sydney Morning Herald*, August 1997.

186. Brown, Malcolm. "Cult Woman Defends Pebble." *Sydney Morning Herald*, June 29, 2005.

187. Enroth, Ronald M. *Churches that Abuse*. Michigan: Zondervan, 1993.

188. Watts, Kristen. "Lifetime of Faith Ends in Torment." *The West Australian*, June 1998.

189. *The 9/11 Commission Report*. Chapter 2, Page 48, Paragraph 4.

190. Malone, David. "Bin Laden's Plan, The project for the New Al Qaeda Century," Bloomington, IN: Traffor Publishing, 2001.

191. Rosenthal, Justine A. ed., "Reversing Islamic Radicalization." *State of the Struggle: Report on the Battle against Global Terrorism*. Washington, D.C.: Brookings Institution Press, February 2007.

192. "Bin Laden Has Been Linked to a Web of Terror For Years." *The Providence Journal*, Boston 2001.

193. "The Next Mahdi." Islamfortoday.com, August 2007.

194. Kent, Steven. "Management Training Damages Employees." *The Cult Observer* (March/April 1997): Vol. 13, No. 2.

195. *ABC Four Corners*, October 1993; "A Current Affair," Channel 9, April 1993; *The Daily Telegraph*, April 1996.

196. Akhtar, Salman. "The Psychodynamic Dimension of Terrorism." *Psychiatric Annals* (June 1999): Vol. 29, No. 6, pp. 350–355.

197. Milgram, Stanley. "Behavioral Study of Obedience." *Journal of Abnormal Social Psychology* (1963) 67:371-8.

198. "IDF kills 20 Palestinians, including 6 children, in Gaza and West Bank." Haaretz.com, February 2008.

199. Ghosh, Bobby. "Inside the Mind of an Iraqi Suicide Bomber." *Time*, June 2005.

200. Johmll, Kim. "Pastor Given Twenty Years for Sexual Abuse." *Japan Today*, February 2006.

201. Speckhard, Anne. "Understanding Suicide Terrorism: Countering Human Bombs and Their Senders." *Topics in Terrorism: Toward a Transatlantic Consensus on the Nature of the Threat* (Volume I), Eds. Jason S. Purcell & Joshua D. Weintraub. Atlantic Council Publication 2005.

202. The Fort Wayne (Indiana) *News-Sentinel*, 1990.

203. Abdullaev, Nabi. "Cults Promises to Resurrect Beslan Children." *Moscow Times*, 2005.

204. Rout, Milanda. "Questions About Steiner's Classroom." *The Australian*, July 2007.

205. "Sect's Meeting Draws Criticism." *The Gazette*, Montréal, February 1995.

206. Arutz Sheva, *Israel National News.com*. July 2006.

207. Volkan, Vamik D. *Suicide Bombers*. Charlottesville, VA: University Press of. Virginia, 1990.

208. Stohl, Rachel. "Children Used as Soldiers in Iraq." The Center for Defense Information, November 2002: Washington ,D.C.

209. Ha'aretz Staff and Agencies. "16 year old Rishon Bomber was Youngest to Strike Israel." Tel Aviv, June 9, 2002 cited in *Child Abuse: The New Islamic Cult of Martyrdom* by Justus Reid Weiner.

210. Swami, Praveen. "Jehadi Groups Set Up Recruitment of Children." *The Hindu*, Chennai, September 9, 2003.

211. Erlanger, Steven. "Suicide Blast Kills 4 at Tel Aviv Market: 16 year old Bomber injures 32 others at Outdoor Stalls." *San Francisco Chronicle*, November 2, 2004.

212. O'Shea, Chiade. "Nato accuses Taliban of using children in suicide missions." *The Guardian*, June 2007.

213. Abawi, Atia. "Teen trained to be suicide bomber feels tricked." *CNN. com*, January 2009.

214. "Suicide Bombers' Mother Elected to Palestinian Parliament; 'Mother of the Struggle' Says She Would Sacrifice Remaining Sons for Jihad." *ABC*

News, January 2006.

215. "The Exploitation of Children for Terrorist Purposes." *Likud Nederland*, January 2003.

216. Lyall, Sarah. "British Intelligence Chief Sharpens Terrorism Warning." *New York Times*, November 2007.

217. Benard, Cheryl. "A Future for the Young; Options for helping Middle Eastern Youth Escape the Trap of Radicalization." Paper presented at Rand's Initiative on Middle Eastern Youth, September 2005.

218. Letter from a parent concerned about the plight of a mentally ill child.

219. Moore, Matthew. "Suspect Is Mentally Disturbed." *Sydney Morning Herald*, November 2005.

220. Pollard, Ruth. "They Sought Help But Got Exorcism and the Bible." *The Sydney Morning Herald*, March 2008.

221. Ibid.

222. Ibid.

223. Ibid.

224. *www.cchr.org.*

225. "Scientology Attacks on Psychiatry Escalate." *The Cult Observer* (1996): Vol. 13, No. 4, 5.

226. Wallsten, Peter and Diane Rado, "Bill seeks to strip authority from HRS." *St Petersburg Times*, April 4, 1996.

227. Leppard, David. "M15 Fears Jihadis Will Use Mentally Ill as Suicide Bombers." *The Sunday Times*, May 2008.

228. "Terrorists Target the Mentally Ill as Useful." *LA Times–Washington Post*, July 2008.

229. Leppard, David. "M15 Fears Jihadis Will Use Mentally Ill as Suicide Bombers." *The Sunday Times*, May 2008.

Chapter Six

230. Gartenstein-Ross, Daveed. *My Year Inside Radical Islam*. USA: Jeremy P. Tarcher/Penguin, 2008.

231. Norberg-Hodge, Helena. "The March of the Monoculture." ISEC (International Society for Ecology & Culture).

232. Morgan, Brittany. "I was Trapped in a Therapy Cult." *Mademoiselle*, Conde Nast Publications Inc., 1999.

233. Husain, Ed. *The Islamist: Why I Joined Radical Islam in Britain: What I Saw Inside and Why I Left*. United Kingdom: Penguin, 2007.

234. Bunting, Madeleine. "We Were Brothers." *The Guardian*, May 2007.

235. Asahi, Shinbun, September 10, 1997.

236. Hall, John R., Philip D. Schuyler, Sylvaine Trinh. *Apocalypse Observed.*

London: Taylor & Francis, January 2000.

237. Tourish, Dennis Dr. "The London Bombings: The Dark Side of Group Dynamics." *The Irish Times*, July 2005.

238. Blossfeld, Hans-Peter, Erik Klijzing, Melinda Mills, Karin Kurz, Eds. *Globalization, Uncertainty and Youth in Society.* USA: Routledge June 2005.,

239. CalTech Counseling Center at California Institute of Technology, www.counseling.caltech.edu/articles/cults.html.

Chapter Seven

240. Braithwaite, David. "Scientology Cited in Killings." *The Sydney Morning Herald*, July 2007. (Note: In July 2008, the woman was found not guilty on the grounds of mental illness. Judge Michael Grove of the New South Wales Supreme Court said that the woman's father's association with Scientology did not affect the treatment of his daughter's mental illness. The judge found that the woman's father had sought psychiatric help for his daughter's psychotic condition despite his apparent belief in Scientology which is reluctant to recognize the benefits of such treatment.)

241. Leiby, Richard. "A Couch Tom Cruise Won't Jump On. Actor Lambastes Psychiatry on 'Today." *Washington Post*, June 25, 2005.

242. Bachelard, Michael. "Judge's Ruling Warns Brethren." *The Melbourne Age*, February 2007.

243. Australasian Legal Information Institute, 2002.

244. Amnesty International Annual Report, 2002.

245. "The Impact of UK Anti-Terror Laws on Freedom of Expression." Submission to ICJ Panel of Eminent Jurists on Terrorism, Counter-Terrorism and Human Rights, London, April 2006.

246. "Conviction with Compassion: A Report on Freedom of Religion and Belief," The Joint Standing Committee on Foreign Affairs, Defence and Trade, Tabled in the Parliament of Australia, November 27, 2000.

247. "Polygamist Cult's Action Boggle Mind." *The Detroit News*, April 2008.

248. Hansard Record of Parliament of New South Wales, Australia: Speaker: The Hon Stephen Mutch. November 1992.

249. Bachelard, Michael. "Rudd in Brethren About Face." *The Melbourne Age*, May 2008.

250. Hussein, Shakira. "The Elusive Brethren." newmatilda.com, May 2008.

251. Corlew, Jen. "Free Speech Victory as Charges Against Teen Anti-Scientology Protestor Dropped." *Liberty*, May 2008.

252. ABC 7 News, The DenverChannel.com.

253. "Cult Leader Jailed for More Sexual Abuse." *The Sydney Morning Her-*

ald, August 2007, The Melbourne Age, August 2007.

254. *The Australian*, October 14, 1998.

255. For a discussion this issue, see "The Exclusive Brethren and the Rights of Children," Radio National Transcript, *The Religion Report*, www.abc.net.au/rn/religionreport/stories/2007/1871059.htm. March 14, 2007.

256. Bachelard, Michael. "Judge's Ruling Warns Brethren." *The Melbourne Age*, February 2007.

257. Bachelard, Michael. "Sect Told Girl: Banish Your Dad." *Sydney Morning Herald,* December 2006.

258. Lichfield, John. " France bans websites promoting anorexia 'cult'." *The Independent*, April 2008.

259. Tabor, James D. and Eugene V. Gallagher. *Why Waco? Cults and the Battle for Religious Freedom in America*. California: University of California Press, July 1995.

260. Kohn, Rachel. "The Spirit of Things." *ABC Radio National,* February 2006.

261. "German Authorities Consider Outlawing Scientology." *Catholic Newsagency,* December 2007.

262. Villagran, Miguel. "Germany's Battle Against Scientology." *Time*, December 2007.

263. Briton, Bob. "Sects and Cults: Thriving Trade in Misery." *The Guardian,* April 2008.

264. Felps, Paula. "The Alluring Life Offered by the World's Largest 'Multimarketing' Business Closely Represents a Sham." *Weekly Wire*, July 1998.

265. "Widow of Bomber 'Abhors' Attack." *BBC News,* September 2005.

Chapter Eight

266. "UN General Assembly, Uniting against terrorism : recommendations for a global counter-terrorism strategy : report of the Secretary-General." April 27, 2006, A/60/825, available at: http://www.unhcr.org/refworld/docid/4786248b7.html.

267. Evans, Gareth. "Responding to Terrorism: A Global Stocktake." Keynote Address to Calouste Gulbenkian Conference on Terrorism and International Relations, Lisbon, October 25, 2005.

268. Gartenstein-Ross, Daveed. *My Year Inside Radical Islam,* USA: Jeremy P. Tarcher/Penguin 2008.

269. Spritzer, Dinah A. "Can Britain Deprogram the Radicalism of its Muslim Population?" *JTA,* February 2009.

270. See Appendix A for The Doomsday Document.

271. Cole, Juan. "Al Qaeda, Doomsday Document and Psychological Manipulation." Paper presented at "Genocide and Terrorism: Probing the Mind

of the Perpetrator." Yale Center for Genocide Studies, New Haven, April 9, 2003.

272. Daly, Sara and Scott Gerwehr. "Al-Qaida: Terrorist Selection and Recruitment." *McGraw-Hill Homeland Security Handbook* (2006): Chapter 5, p. 73-89. https://www.rand.org/pubs/reprints/2006/RAND_RP1214.pdf.

273. Balsano, Aida B. "The Role of Developmental Assets and Youth Civic Engagement in Promoting Positive Development Among Youth" in *Options for Helping Middle Eastern Youth Escape the Trap of Radicalization*. RAND's Initiative on Middle Eastern Youth, 2005.

274. Walker, John. "American Indoctrinated with Cult Mind Control Techniques by Taliban." Statement by cult expert, Steve Hassan, December 2001, published on his website, www.freedomofmind.com/stevehassan/presskit/releases/12-03-01.htm.

275. White, Mark. "Brainwashing: The Terror Leader's Tool." *Sky News*, May 2008.

276. Mirza, Syed Kanran. "What is Islamic Terrorism and How Could it be Defeated?" *Islam Watch*.

277. Weiner, Justus Reid. "Child Abuse: The New Islamic Cult of Martyrdom." South Asia Terrorism Portal, 2007.

278. www.islamfortoday.com/terrorism.htm.

279. Abdullah. "Worldwide Muslim Condemnation of Terrorism." www.whyIslam.org.

280. "Muslims Against Terrorism." www.islamfortoday.com .

281. Benard, Cheryl. "A Future for the Young; Options for helping Middle Eastern Youth Escape the Trap of Radicalization." Paper presented at RAND's Initiative on Middle Eastern Youth, September 2005.

282. World Security Institute, Brussels.

283. "Al-Hayat Al-Jadida," January 4, 2007 reported in the *American Thinker*, April 2008.

284. Ibid.

285. Houlihan, Liam. "Islamic Pro-terrorism Hate Film Gets PG Rating." *The Sunday Telegraph*, April 2007.

286. Phillips, Melanie. "Faking a Killing." *Standpoint Online*, July 2008.

287. Barducci, Dr. R. "Surge of Terrorism in Algeria Intensifies Debate Over Government's National Reconciliation Policy." *Memri Enquiry and Analysis*. Series No. 392.

288. "Implementing the UN General Assembly's Counter-Terrorism Strategy: Addressing Youth Radicalisation in the Mediterranean Region. Lessons Learned, Best Practices and Recommendations." The Istituto Affari Internazionali (IAI) and the Center for Global Counter Terrorism Co-operation (Center), Rome, July 11-12, 2007.

289. http://www.fiqhcouncil.org.

290. Marcus, Itamar. "Palestinian Authority Renews Efforts to Have Palestinian Children Die in Confrontations." *Palestinian Media Watch Bulletin*, October 1, 2002.

291. Ghosh, Bobby. "Professor of Death." *Time Magazine*, October 2005.

292. "Dissuading Groups from Resorting to Terrorism or Supporting It; Uniting Against Terrorism." A United Nations Report, May 2006.

293. Tripathi, Salil. "Economics and Politics: Debunking the Poverty-Terrorism Myth." *The Asian Wall Street Journal*, February 2005.

294. Mezey Mathy Doval (Editor), Sherry A. Greenberg (Editor), Diane O'Neill McGivern (Editor), Eileen Sullivan-Marx (Editor). *Nurse Practitioners: Evolution of Advanced Practise*. United States: Springer Publishing, 2003.

295. Los Angeles Police Department, Los Angeles, California, 2005.

296. http://john-barnett.blogspot.com/2007/03/needs-part-2-need-to-belong.html.

297. Bunting, Madeleine. "We Were Brothers." *The Guardian*, May 2007.

298. Comments adapted from Prime Minister Jan Peter Balkenende's address at the two-day ministerial meeting of the Organisation for Security and Cooperation in Europe (OSCE) in Maastricht. December 2003.

299. Yahmid, Hadi. "Failed Policy, Marginalization Sparked Riots." *Islam On Line*, November 2005.

300. Ibid.

301. "Implementing the UN General Assembly's Counter-Terrorism Strategy: Addressing Youth Radicalisation in the Mediterranean Region. Lessons Learned, Best Practices and Recommendations." The Istituto Affari Internazionali (IAI) and the Center for Global Counter Terrorism Co-operation (Center). Rome, July 11-12, 2007.

302. Comments adapted from Prime Minister Jan Peter Balkenende's address at the two-day ministerial meeting of the Organisation for Security and Cooperation in Europe (OSCE) in Maastricht. December 2003.

Epilogue

303. Rosenthal, Justine A., ed. *State of the Struggle: Report on the Battle against Global Terrorism*. Washington, D.C.: Brookings Institution Press, February 2007.

304. al Saleh, Huda. "Saudi Arabia: Internet Most Popular Terrorist Recruitment Method – Official." Asharq Alawsat, May 2007.

305. "1/3 of UK's Muslim Students Support 'Jihad.'" *CBNews.com*, July 2008.

306. In January 2008 Ahmad Syafii Maarif was one of the seven 2008 Ramon Magsaysay (RM) awardees honored by the Philippine-based RM

Award Foundation (RMAF). Maarif was the awardee for Peace and International Understanding, a category that "recognizes contributions to the advancement of friendship, tolerance, peace, and solidarity as the foundations for sustainable development within and across countries."

307. "Psychology professor David Canter on motives for terrorism." *CBC News*, April 2007.

Bibliography

Abuza, Zachary. *Funding Terrorism in Southeast Asia: The Financial Network of Al Qaeda and Jemaah Islamiyah.* Seattle, Washington: The National Bureau of Asian Research, 2003.

Akhtar, Salman. *"The Psychodynamic Dimension of Terrorism."* Psychiatric Annals, (June 1999): vol. 29, no. 6, 350–355.

Albertini, Tamara. "The Seductiveness of Certainty: The Destruction of Islam's Intellectual Legacy by the Fundamentalists." *Philosophy East and West,* (October 2003): vol. 53, no. 4, 455-470.

Arendt, Hannah and Amos Elon. *Eichmann in Jerusalem: A Report on the Banality of Evil.* New York: Penguin (Non-Classics), 1994.

Aron, Raphael. *Cults: Too Good To Be True.* Melbourne, Australia: Harper Collins, 1999.

Arendt, Hannah. *The Origins of Totalitarianism.* New York: Harcourt, Brace & Co., 1951.

Aronson, Elliot, Timothy D. Wilson, and Robin M. Akert. *Social Psychology: The Heart and the Mind.* New York: Harper, Collins, 2002.

Bachelard, Michael. *Behind the Exclusive Brethren.* Victoria, Australia: Scribe Publications, 2008.

Barkun, Michael. *Religion and the Racist Right: The Origins of the Christian Identity Movement.* Chapel Hill, NC: University of North Carolina Press, 1996.

Bartoletti, Susan Campbell. *Hitler Youth: Growing Up In Hitler's Shadow.* New York: Scholastic, 2005.

Bell, Bowyer. "Psychology of Leaders of Terrorist Groups." *International Journal of Group Tensions* (1982): 12: 84-104.

Bongar, Bruce ed., Lisa M. Brown, Larry E. Beutler, James N. Breckenridge, and Philip G. Zimbardo. *Psychology of Terrorism.* (2006): USA: Oxford University Press.

Booth, Leo. *When God Becomes a Drug: Breaking the Chains of Religious Addiction and Abuse.* New York: J.P. Tarcher/Perigee, 1991.

Borum, Randy. *Psychology of Terrorism.* Tampa: University of South Florida, 2004.

Burton, Anthony. *Revolutionary Volence: The Theories*. New York: Crane, Russak, 1978.

Bushart, Howard L., Myra Edwards Barnes. *Soldiers of God: White Supremacists and Their Holy War for America*. New York: Kensington Publishing Corp, 1998.

Conway, Flo and Jim Sigelman. *Snapping: America's Epidemic of Sudden Personality Change*. New York: Stillpoint Press, 1978 updated 1995, second edition.

Crenshaw, Martha. "The Logic of Terrorism: Terrorist Behavior as a Product of Strategic Choice," in Walter Reich, ed. *Origins of Terrorism* (1998).

Crenshaw, Martha. "The Psychology of Terrorism: An Agenda for the 21st Century." *International Society of Political Psychology* (June 2000): vol. 21, no. 2, 405–420.

Crenshaw, Martha, ed. *Terrorism in Context*. University Park: Pennsylvania Street University Press, 1995.

Daly, M. & M. Wilson. "The Evolutionary Psychology of Male Violence," in J. Archer, ed. (1994): 253-288.

Enroth, Ronald. *Churches that Abuse*. Grand Rapids, Michigan: Zondervan, 1992.

Ferracuti, Franco. "Psychiatric Aspects of Italian Left Wing and Right Wing Terrorism." Paper presented at the VII World Congress of Psychiatry, Vienna, Austria, 1983.

Ferracuti, Franco. "A Sociopsychiatric Interpretation of Terrorism." *Annals of American Academy of Political & Social Science* (982463): 129-41.

Ferrell, Jeff. "Against the Law: Anarchist Criminology," In Brian D. MacLean and Dragan Milovanovic, eds. *Thinking Critically About Crime*. Richmond: British Columbia: Collective Press, 1997.

Ferrell, Jeff. "Anarchist Criminology and Social Justice," pp. 91-108 in Bruce Arrigo, ed. *Social justice/Criminal Justice* (1999).

Forsyth, Donelson R. *Group Dynamics*, 3rd edition. Belmont, CA: Brooks/Cole, 1999.

Furnish, Timothy. "The Man Who Would Be Mahdi." *Middle East Quarterly* (Spring 2002), www.mahdiwatch.org. (Accessed December 1 2008).

Galvin, Deborah. "The Female Terrorist: A Socio-psychological Perspective." *Behavioral Science & Law* (1983): 1: 19-32.

Gartenstein-Ross, Daveed. *My Year Inside Radical Islam*. USA: Jeremy P. Tarcher/Penguin, 2008.

Georges-Abeyie, D. & L. Hass. "Propaganda by Deed: Defining Terrorism." *The Justice Reporter* (1982) 2: 1-7. Toronto.

Giduck, John. *Terror At Beslan: A Russian Tragedy with Lessons for America's Schools*. Colorado: Archangel Group Inc., 2005.

Grossman D. *On Killing, The Psychological Cost of Learning to Kill in War and*

Society. New York: Little Brown, 1995.

Gupta, Dipak K. *Path to Collective Madness: A Study in Social Order and Political Pathology*. Westport, CT.: Praeger, 2001.

Hacker, Frederick. *Crusaders, Criminals, Crazies: Terror and Terrorists in our Time*. New York: Norton, 1996.

Hall, John R., Philip D. Schuyler, Sylvaine Trinh. *Apocalypse Observed*. London: Taylor & Francis, January 2000.

Hamilton-Byrne, Sarah. *Unseen, Unheard, Unknown*. Victoria, Australia: Penguin Books Australia, 1995.

Hassan, Steven. *Combatting Cult Mind Control*. Rochester, Vermont: Inner Traditions International: October 1990.

Hassan, Steven. *Releasing the Bonds: Empowering People to Think for Themselves*. Somerville, MA: Freedom of Mind Press, 2000.

Heck, Alfons. *A Child of Hitler*. New York: Bantam Books, 1985.

Hoffman, Bruce. *Inside Terrorism*. New York: Columbia University Press, 1998.

Holmes, Richard. *Acts of War: The Behavior of Men in Battle*. New York: Free Press, 1986.

Horgan, John. *The Psychology of Terrorism*. London and New York: Routledge, 2005.

Howard & Reid Sawyer, eds. *Terrorism and Counterterrorism*. New York: McGraw-Hill, 2004.

Hudson, Rex. *Who Becomes a Terrorist and Why*. Guilford: Ct Lyons Press, 1999.

Husain, Ed. *The Islamist: Why I Joined Radical Islam in Britain, What I Saw Inside and Why I Left*. United Kingdom: Penguin, 2007.

Jenkins, J. "Resource Mobilization Theory and the Study of Social Movements." *Annual Review of Sociology* (1983): 9: 527–53.

Joiner, Thomas E. *Why People Die by Suicide*. Cambridge, USA: Harvard University Press, 2007.

Juergensmeyer, M. *Terror in the Mind of God: The Global Rise of Religious Violence*. Berkeley: University of California Press, 2001.

Kaplan, A. "The Psychodynamics of Terrorism." Y. Alexander & J. Gleason (eds.) *Behavioral and Quantitative Perspectives on Terrorism* (1981).

Kaplan, David E. and Andrew Marshall. *The Cult at the End of the World: The Terrifying Story of the Aum Doomsday Cult*. New York: Crown, 1996.

Kater, Michael H. *Hitler Youth*. Cambridge: Harvard University Press, 2004.

Klein, Aaron. *Schmoozing with Terrorists: From Hollywood to the Holy Land Jihadists Reveal their Global Plans*. California: WND Books, 2008.

Kohlmann, Evan F. "The Role of Islamic Charities in International Terrorist Recruitment and Financing," DIIS Working Paper No. 2006/7, Copenhagen: Danish Institute for International Studies, 2006.

Kraemer, E. *A Philosopher Looks at Terrorism.* Nyatepe-Coo, A. & Zeisler-Vralsted, D., eds. *Understanding Terrorism* (2004): 113-131.

Laqueur, Walter. *No End to War: Terrorism in the Twenty-first Century.* New York : Continuum, 2003.

Laqueur, Walter. *The New Terrorism.* New York: Oxford University Press, 1999.

Layton, Deborah. *Seductive Poison.* California: Random House, 1998.

Leeman, Richard. *The Rhetoric of Terrorism.* New York: Greenwood Press, 1991.

Lemert, Charles and Anthony Elliot. *Deadly Worlds: The Emotional Costs of Globalization.* Oxford: Rowman and Littlefield Publishers, 2006.

Long, David. *The Anatomy of Terrorism.* New York: Free Press, 1990.

Marlowe, Laura. "A Fiery Cleric's Defense of Jihad," *Time,* January 15, 1996. See Bruce Hoffman. *Inside Terrorism.* New York: Columbia University Press, 1998.

Merari, A. "The Readiness to Kill and Die: Suicidal Terrorism in the Middle East." in W. Reich, ed. *Origins of Terrorism* (1990).

Milgram, Stanley. "Behavioral Study of Obedience," *Journal of Abnormal and Social Psychology* (1963): vol. 67, pp. 371–378.

Moghaddam, Fathali. "The Staircase to Terrorism: A Psychological Exploration," in *American Psychologist* (2005): Vol. 60(2), 161-169.

Morgan, Stephen J. *The Mind of a Terrorist Fundamentalist: The Psychology of Terror Cults.* Cincinatti: Awe-Struck E-Books, 2001

Moscovici, Serge. "Social Influence and Conformity," in G. Linzey and Elliot Aronson, eds. *Handbook of Social Psychology* (1985): 3rd ed. 347–412.

Mullen, B. "Atrocity as a Function of Lynch Mob Composition: A Self-Attention Perspective." Michigan: *Personality and Social Psychology Bulletin* (1983): vol. 12, 187-197.

Nassar, J. *Globalization and Terrorism.* Lanham, MD: Rowman & Littlefield, 2005.

Nasuti, Guy. "The Hitler Youth: An Effective Organization for Total War," www.militaryhistoryonline.com/wwii/articles/effectiveorganization.aspx (accessed December 1, 2008).

Nyatepe-Coo, A. "Economic Implications of Terrorism," pp. 77-89 in Nyatepe-Coo, A. & Zeisler-Vralsted, D., eds. *Understandig Terrorism* (2004).

Olsson, Dr Peter. *Malignant Pied Pipers of Our Time: A Psychological Study of Destructive Cult Leaders from Rev. Jim Jones to Osama bin Laden.* Frederick, MD: Publish America, 2005.

O'Sullivan, N. *Terrorism, Ideology, and Revolution.* Boulder, Colarado: West-view, 1986.

Pape, Robert. *Dying to Win: The Strategic Logic of Suicide Terrorism.* New York: Random House, 2005.

Passmore, K. *Fascism: A Very Short Introduction.* New York: Oxford University Press, 2002.

Paz, Reuven. "The Islamic Legitimacy of Palestinian Suicide Terrorism," in

Countering Suicide Terrorism. (2007): pp 61-62.

Post, Jerrold M. *The Mind of the Terrorist, The Psychology of Terrorism from the IRA to al-Qaeda.* United Kingdom: Palgrave Macmillan, 2008.

Post, Jerrold M. "Terrorist Psycho-Logic: Terrorist Behavior as a Product of Psychological Forces," in Walter Reich, ed. *Origins of Terrorism: Psychologies, Ideologies, Theologies, States of Mind.* (1998): 25-40.

Post, Jerrold M. 'Terrorist Psych-Logic: Terrorist Behaviour as a Product of Psychological Forces" in W. Reich, ed. *Origins of Terrorism: Psychologies, Ideologies, States of Mind* (1990).

Ranstorp, Magnus. "Terrorism in the Name of Religion." *Journal of International Affairs* (1996): 121-36. New York: School of International and Public Affairs at Columbia University.

Rapoport, David & Yonah Alexander, eds. *The Morality of Terrorism: Religious and Secular Justifications.* New York: Pergamon Press, 1982.

Rapoport, David. "Fear and trembling: Terrorism in three religious traditions." *American Political Science Review* (1984): 78(3): 668-72. Washington.

Reader, Ian. "Imagined Persecution: Aum Shinrikyô, Millennialism, and the Legitimation of Violence." In *Millennialism, Persecution, and Violence: Historical Cases*, ed. Catherine Wessinger (2000), 158-82.

Reich, Walter. "Understanding Terrorist Behavior: The Limits and Opportunities of Psychological Inquiry," in *Origins of Terrorism* (1990).

Reiterman, Tim and John Jacobs. *Raven: The Untold Story of Rev. Jim Jones and His People.* United States: Dutton Adult, 1982.

Robbins, Thomas. *Cults, Converts, and Charisma: The Sociology of New Religious Movements.* Newbury Park, CA: Sage Publications, 1988.

Rosenthal, Justine A., (ed.), *State of the Struggle: Report on the Battle against Global Terrorism,* Washington, D.C: Brookings Institution Press, February 2007.

Ross, Jeffrey Ian. "Beyond the Conceptualization of Terrorism: A Psychological-Sttructural Model" in C. Summers & E. Mardusen, eds. *Collective Violence*, 1999. New York: Rowen & Littlefield.

Ruby, Charles. "Are Terrorists Mentally Deranged?" *Analyses of Social Issues and Public Policy* (2002): 2(1): 15-26.

Russell, Charles & Bowman Miller. "Profile of a Terrorist." *Terrorism: An International Journal* (1977): 1(1): 17-34.

Samways, Louise. *Dangerous Persuaders.* Australia: Penguin Books, 1994. Updated as an E-book in 2007.

Silke, Andrew. "Cheshire-Cat Logic: The Recurring Theme of Terrorist Abnormality in Psychological Research," *Psychology, Crime and Law,* vol. 4, pp. 51–59.

Simonsen, C. & J. Spindlove. *Terrorism Today: The Past, the Players, the Future.* Upper Saddle River, NJ: Prentice Hall, 2007.

Singer, Margaret Thaler and Janja Lalich. *Cults in Our Midst: The Hidden Menace in Our Everyday Lives.* San Francisco: Jossey-Bass, 1995.

Snow, Robert L. *Deadly Cults: The Crimes of True Believers.* Westport, CT: Greenwood Pub. Group, 2003.

Snowden, L. & B. Whitsel, eds. *Terrorism: Research, Readings, and Realities.* NJ: Prentice Hall, 2005.

Stahelski, Anthony Ph.D. "Terrorists Are Made, Not Born: Creating Terrorists Using Social Psychological Conditioning." *Washington: Journal of Homeland Security,* March 2004.

Stern, Jessica. *The Ultimate Terrorists.* Cambridge: Harvard University Press, 1999.

Strentz, Thomas. "A Terrorist Psychological Profile." *Law Enforcement Bulletin* (1988) 57: 11-18.

Swetman, Michael S. and Yonah Alexander. *Osama Bin Laden's Al Qaeda: A Profile of a Terrorist Network.* New York: Transnational Publishers, 2002.

Tabor, James D. and Eugene V. Gallagher. *Why Waco?* USA: University of California Press, 1995.

Taheri, Amir. *Holy Terror: Inside the World of Islamic Terrorism.* Bethesda, MD: Adler & Adler, 1987.

Tajfel, Henri, ed. *Social Identity and Intergroup Relations.* Cambridge: Cambridge University Press, 1982.

Tourish, Dennis and Tim Wohlforth. *On the Edge: Political Cults Right and Left.* Armonk, New York: M.E. Sharpe, 2000.

Waller, James. *Becoming Evil: How Ordinary People Commit Genocide and Mass Killing.* England: Oxford University Press, 2002.

Wilkinson, Richard. *The Impact of Inequality: How to Make Sick Societies Healthier.* London and New York: Routledge, 2005.

Williams, Phil. "Warning Indicators, Terrorist Finances, and Terrorist Adaptation." *Strategic Insights* (2005): Vol. IV, No. 1.

Wilson, E. *Sociobiology: The New Synthesis.* Cambridge: Harvard University Press, 1975.

Wooden, Kenneth. *Children of Jonestown.* New York: McGraw-Hill, 1981.

Wright, Stuart A., ed. *Armageddon in Waco: Critical Perspectives on the Branch Davidian Conflict.* Chicago: University of Chicago Press, 1995.

Young, Jock. *The Exclusive Society.* Thousand Oaks, CA: Sage, 1999.

Zimbardo, Phillip G. "The Human Choice: Individuation, Reason, and Order Versus Deindividuation, Impulse, and Chaos," in W. T. Arnold and D. Levine, eds. Nebraska Symposium on Motivation (1969) vol. 17. 237–307.

Zimbardo, Phillip G. *The Lucifer Effect: Understanding How Good People Turn Evil,* USA: Random House, March 2007.

Index

Order of the Solar Temple, 18–19, 41
Osho, 16. *See also* Rajneesh, Bhagwan Shree
out-group. *See* in-group *vs.* out-group

Packer, James, 69
Palestinians, 22, 69, 81, 113, 160–61. *See also under* suicide bombers
   child suicide bombers and soldiers, 113, 115–19, 163
parenting, 101
parents sending children to be suicide bombers, 117
Paris riots, 166
Patriotic Union of Kurdistan (PUK), 115–16
patriotism, 70
Pedahzur, Ami, 50, 64, 71
Pell, George, 103–4
Peoples Temple. *See* Jones, Jim; Jonestown tragedy of 1978
Pereira, Ray, 114–15
perfectionists, 65
personality breakdown, 108–12
personality disorders among terrorists, 89–90
personality profile in cults *vs.* religions, 75–76
phobias, creation of, 48
Piraino, Genna, 105
planned spontaneity. *See* mystical manipulation
polarization. *See* demonization; "good" *vs.* "evil"
polygamy, 138, 142
Popular Front for the Liberation of Palestine (PFLP), 116
poverty and terrorism, 87–88
prisons, 156
"Pro-Ana" movement, 144
propaganda, 50, 159. *See also* information control
proselytizing, 56–57
pseudo-personality, 52, 53, 55
psychiatry, 136–37
psychological manipulation
   See mind control
psychopathology among terrorists. *See* cults; mentally ill persons; personality
      disorders among terrorists
purity. *See also* "good" *vs.* "evil"
   demand for, 40–41, 65

Quilliam Foundation, 153–54
Qur'an. *See* Koran